THE
GIFT OF
DEATH

RELIGION AND POSTMODERNISM
A Series Edited by Mark C. Taylor

THE
GIFT OF
DEATH

JACQUES DERRIDA

TRANSLATED BY
DAVID WILLS

THE UNIVERSITY OF CHICAGO PRESS
CHICAGO & LONDON

JACQUES DERRIDA is *directeur d'études* at the Ecole des Hautes
Etudes in Sciences Sociales. The University of Chicago Press has
published eleven of his books in English, including, most recently,
Given Time and *Memoirs of the Blind*. David Wills is professor of French
and chair of the Department of French and Italian at Louisiana State
University.

Originally published as *Donner la mort* in *L'éthique du don, Jacques Derrida
et la pensée du don*, by Métailié-Transition, © Transition, Paris, 1992.

The University of Chicago Press, Chicago 60637
The University of Chicago Press, Ltd., London
© 1995 by The University of Chicago
All rights reserved. Published 1995
Printed in the United States of America
04 03 02 01 00 99 98 97 96 95   1 2 3 4 5
ISBN: 0-226-14305-8 (cloth)

Library of Congress Cataloging-in-Publication Data

Derrida, Jacques.
    [Donner la mort. English]
    The gift of death / Jacques Derrida : translated by David Wills.
        p.   cm.
    Includes bibliographical references.
    1. Generosity.   2. Gifts.   3. Responsibility.   I. Title.
    B2430-D483D6613   1995
    194—dc20   94-28893

CONTENTS

TRANSLATOR'S PREFACE

The French text of this essay, entitled "Donner la mort," was published in a collection of papers from a conference held at Royaumont in December 1990, on "The Ethics of the Gift" (ed. Jean-Michel Rabaté and Michael Wetzel, *L'Ethique du don: Jacques Derrida et la pensée du don* [Paris: Transition, 1992]). "Donner la mort" is not, however, the paper Derrida delivered at that conference, that being part of a volume that was at the time already destined for publication (*Donner le temps* [Paris: Galilée, 1991]) and now translated as *Given Time. 1. Counterfeit Money*, translation by Peggy Kamuf (Chicago: University of Chicago Press, 1992). Neither is *The Gift of Death* intended, as it might seem, to be the second volume of *Given Time;* it is instead a different reflection within a series on the question of the gift.

The French title "Donner la mort" plays on the ordinary sense of *donner*, meaning "to give," and the idiomatic sense of this expression, which is "to put to death," as in *se donner la mort,* "to commit suicide." In translating Derrida's title with the noun phrase I seek to have heard in it (or behind it) the English expression "kiss of death." In the text I have tried to follow the idea of "giving" or "granting" wherever possible, but I have used "to put to death" when comprehensibility so demands, sometimes adding the French for mnemonic purposes. Whenever "to put to death" is used, however, the reader should also hear the sense of "giving."

The Gift of Death starts from an analysis of an essay by the Czech philosopher Jan Patočka, who, along with Vaclav Havel and Jiri Hajek, was one of three spokesmen for the Charta 77 human rights declaration of 1977. He died of a brain hemorrhage after eleven hours of police interrogation on 13 March 1977. A selection of Patočka's essays in English, as well as full biographical and bibliographical details, appear in Erazim Kohák, *Jan Patočka: Philosophy and Selected Writings* (Chicago: University of Chicago Press, 1989), and a translation of the *Heretical Essays on the Philosophy of History* is due to appear with Open Court Publishing (Chicago) in 1995. The collective "Charter 77 Manifesto" appears in *Telos* 31 (1977).

I acknowledge with gratitude the assistance provided by a Louisiana State University Center for French and Francophone Studies Summer Research Grant in the preparation of this translation.

ONE

Secrets of European Responsibility

In one of his *Heretical Essays on the Philosophy of History*[1] Jan Patočka relates secrecy,[2] or more precisely the mystery of the sacred, to responsibility. He opposes one to the other; or rather underscores their heterogeneity. Somewhat in the manner of Levinas he warns against an experience of the sacred as an enthusiasm or fervor for fusion, cautioning in particular against a form of demonic rapture that has as its effect, and often as its first intention, the removal of responsibility, the loss of the sense or consciousness[3] of responsibility. At the same time Patočka wants to distinguish religion from

1. *"La civilisation technique est-elle une civilisation de déclin, et pourquoi?"* ("Is Technological Civilization a Civilization in Decline, and If So Why?"), in *Essais hérétiques sur la philosophie de l'histoire*, trans. Erika Abrams (Lagrasse: Verdier, 1981; limited Czech edition, Prague: Petlice, 1975). (Citations have been translated from the French edition, to which page numbers also refer.—Trans. note.)

2. In French *le secret* refers both to "a secret" and to the more abstract sense of "secrecy." In general I have used whichever alternative better suits the syntax.—Trans. note.

3. The French *conscience* translates as both "conscience" and "consciousness" in English. I have used either, according to the syntax, often preferring "conscience" rather than to presume to distinguish among the physiological, psychological, or moral senses of the French word, especially because Derrida's analysis of responsibility calls those distinctions into question.—Trans. note.

1

the demonic form of sacralization. What is a religion? Religion presumes access to the responsibility of a free self. It thus implies breaking with this type of secrecy (for it is not of course the only one), that associated with sacred mystery and with what Patočka regularly calls the demonic. A distinction is to be made between the demonic on the one hand (that which confuses the limits among the animal, the human, and the divine, and which retains an affinity with mystery, the initiatory, the esoteric, the secret or the sacred) and responsibility on the other. This therefore amounts to a thesis on the origin and essence of the religious.

Under what conditions can one speak of a religion, in the proper sense of the term, if such a thing exists? Under what conditions can we speak of a history of religion, and first and foremost of the Christian religion? In noting that Patočka refers only to the example of his own religion I do not seek to denounce an omission or establish the guilt of a failure to develop a comparative analysis. On the contrary, it seems necessary to reinforce the coherence of a way of thinking that takes into account the event of Christian mystery as an absolute singularity, a religion par excellence and an irreducible condition for a joint history of the subject, responsibility, and Europe. That is so even if, here and there, the expression "history of religion*s*" appears in the plural, and even if one can only infer from this plural a reference to Judaic, Islamic, and Christian religions alone, those known as religions of the Book.

According to Patočka one can speak of religion only after the demonic secret, and the orgiastic sacred, have been surpassed [*dépassé*, also "outstripped," "outmoded"]. We should let that term retain its essential ambiguity. In the proper sense of the word, religion exists once the secret of the sacred, orgiastic, or demonic mystery has been, if not destroyed, at least integrated, and finally subjected to the sphere of responsibility. The subject of responsibility will be the subject that has managed to make orgiastic or demonic mystery subject to itself; and has done that in order to freely subject itself to the wholly and infinite other that sees without being seen. Religion is responsibility or it is nothing at all. Its history derives its sense entirely from the idea of a *passage* to responsibility. Such a passage involves traversing or enduring the test by means of which the ethical conscience will be delivered of the demonic, the mystagogic and the enthusiastic, of the initiatory and the esoteric. In the authentic sense of the word, religion comes into being the moment that the experience of responsibility extracts itself from that form of secrecy called demonic mystery.

Since the concept of the *daimon* crosses the boundaries separating the human, the animal, and the divine, one will not be surprised to see Patočka recognizing in it a dimension that is essentially that of sexual desire. In what respect does this demonic mystery of desire involve us in a history of responsibility, more precisely in history *as* responsibility?

"The demonic is to be related to responsibility; in the beginning such a relation did not exist" (110). In other words, the demonic is originally defined as irresponsibility, or, if one wishes, as nonresponsibility. It belongs to a space in which there has not yet resounded the injunction to *respond;* a space in which one does not yet hear the call to explain onself [*répondre de soi*], one's actions or one's thoughts, to respond to the other and answer for oneself before the other. The genesis of responsibility that Patočka proposes will not simply describe a history of religion or religiousness. It will be combined with a genealogy of the subject who says "myself," the subject's relation to itself as an instance of liberty, singularity, and responsibility, the relation to self as being before the other: the other in its relation to infinite alterity, one who regards without being seen but also whose infinite goodness *gives* in an experience that amounts to a *gift of death* [*donner la mort*]. Let us for the moment leave that expression in all its ambiguity.

Since this genealogy is also a history of sexuality, it follows the traces of a genius of Christianity that is the history of Europe.[4] For at the center of Patočka's essay the stakes are clearly defined as follows: how to interpret "the *birth* of Europe in the modern sense of the term" (118)? How to conceive of "the expansion of Europe" (119) before and after the Crusades? More radically still, what is it that ails "modern civilization" inasmuch as it is Euro-

4. Cf. René Chateaubriand's *Genius of Christianity* (1802) and reference to Nietzsche in Chapter 4 below.—Trans. note.

pean? Not that it suffers from a particular fault or from a particular form of blindness. Rather, why does it suffer from ignorance of its history, from a failure to assume its responsibility, that is, the memory of its history *as* history of responsibility?

This misunderstanding does not betray an accidental failing on the part of the scholar or philosopher. It is not in fact a sin of ignorance or lack of knowledge. It is not because they don't know [*faute de savoir*] that Europeans do not read their history as a history of responsibility. European historians' misunderstanding of historicity, which is in the first place a misunderstanding of what links historicity to responsibility, is explained on the contrary by the extent to which their historical knowledge occludes, confines, or saturates those questions, grounds, or abysses, naively presuming to totalize or naturalize them, or, what amounts to the same thing, losing themselves in the details. For at the heart of this history there is something of an abyss [*il y a de l'abîme*], an abyss that resists totalizing summary. Separating orgiastic mystery from Christian mystery, this abyss also announces the origin of responsibility.

> Such is the conclusion that the whole essay moves towards: Modern civilization does not just suffer from its own faults, its own myopia, but also from failing to resolve the whole problem of history. But the problem of history cannot be resolved; it must remain a problem. The danger of the present time is that an excess of knowledge of detail might lead us to forget how to look at the question and the grounds that give rise to it.
>
> It might also be that the question of the decline of civilization has been badly put. Civilization does not of itself exist. The question would be rather a matter of knowing if historical man can yet acknowledge history (*přiznávat se k dějinám*). (127)

This last sentence suggests that historicity remains a secret. Historical man does not want to *admit to* historicity, and first and foremost to the abyss that undermines his own historicity.

Two reasons might be given for this resistance to such an admission.

On the one hand, the history of responsibility is tied to a history of religion. But there is always a risk in acknowledging a *history* of responsibility. It is often thought, on the basis of an analysis of the very concepts of responsibility, freedom, or decision, that to be responsible, free, or capable of deciding cannot be something that is acquired, something conditioned or conditional. Even if there is undeniably a history of freedom or responsibility, such a historicity, it is thought, must remain *extrinsic*. It must not touch the essence of an experience that consists precisely in tearing oneself away from one's own historical conditions. What would responsibility be if it were motivated, conditioned, made possible by a history? Although some might think that there is no exercise of responsibility except in a manner that is essentially historical, the classic concept of decision and responsibility seems to exclude from the essence, heart, or proper moment of responsible *decision* all historical connections (whether they be genealogical or not, whether their causality be mechanical or dialectical, or even if they derive from other types of motivation or programming such as those that relate to a psychoanalytic history). It is therefore difficult to *acknowledge* such a historicity and, to the extent that a whole ethics of responsibility often claims to separate itself, as ethics, from religious revelation, it is even more difficult to tie it closely to a history of religion.

On the other hand, if what Patočka says about this historicity is that it must be *admitted to*, implying thereby that it is something difficult to acknowledge, that is because historicity must *remain open* as a problem that is never to be resolved: "the problem of history . . . must remain a problem." The moment the problem were to be resolved that same totalizing closure would determine the end of history: it would bring in the verdict of nonhistoricity itself. History can be neither a decidable object nor a totality capable of being mastered, precisely because it is tied to *responsibility*, to *faith*, and to the *gift*. To *responsibility* in the experience of absolute decisions made outside of knowledge or given norms, made therefore through the very ordeal of the undecidable; to religious *faith* through a form of involvement with the other that is a venture into absolute risk, beyond knowledge and certainty; to the *gift* and to the gift of death that puts me into relation with the transcendence of the other, with God as selfless goodness, and that gives me what it gives me through a new experience of death. Responsibility and faith go together, however paradoxical that might seem to some, and both should, in the same movement, exceed mastery and knowledge. The gift of death would be this marriage of responsibility and faith. History depends on such an excessive beginning [ouverture].

The paradox here plays on *two heterogeneous types of secret:* on the one hand the secret of historicity, what historical man has difficulty acknowledging but which he *must* acknowledge because it concerns his very responsibility; and on the other hand the secret of orgiastic mystery that the history of responsibility has to break with.

An additional complication further overdetermines the breadth or abyss of this experience. Why speak of secrecy where Patočka states that it is historicity that must be acknowledged? This becoming-responsible, that is, this becoming-historical of humankind, seems to be intimately tied to the properly Christian event of *another secret*, or more precisely of a mystery, the *mysterium tremendum:* the terrifying mystery, the dread, fear and trembling of the Christian in the experience of the sacrificial gift. This trembling seizes one at the moment of becoming a person, and the person can become what it is only in being paralyzed [*transie*], in its very singularity, by the gaze of God. Then it sees itself seen by the gaze of another, "a supreme, absolute and inaccessible being who holds us in his hand not by exterior but by interior force" (116).

This passage from exteriority to interiority, but also from the accessible to the inaccessible, assures the transition from Platonism to Christianity. It is held that, starting from a responsibility and ethico-political self of the Platonic type, a mutation occurs as a result of which the Christian self emerges, although such a self remains to be thought through. For this is indeed one of Patočka's *Heretical Essays:* it doesn't fail to note in passing that Christianity has perhaps not yet thought through the very essence of the self whose arrival it nevertheless records. Christianity has not yet accorded such a self the thematic value it deserves: "As for knowing what this person is, such a question has not yet received an adequate thematic development within the perspective of Christianity" (116).

The secret of the *mysterium tremendum* takes over from a heterogeneous secrecy and at the same time breaks with it. This rupture takes the form of either subordination by *incorporation* (one secret subjects or silences the other) or *repression*. The *mysterium tremendum gets carried away [s'emporte]*, in the double sense of the term: it rises *against* another mystery but it rises *on the back [sur le fond] of* a past mystery. In the end [*au fond*] it represses, repressing what remains its foundation [*son fond*]. The secret that the event of Christianity takes to task is at the same time a form of Platonism—or Neoplatonism—which retains something of the thaumaturgical tradition, and the secret of the orgiastic mystery from which Plato tried to deliver philosophy. Hence the history of responsibility is extremely complicated. The history of the responsible self is built upon the heritage and *patrimony* of secrecy, through a chain reaction of ruptures and repressions that assure the very tradition they punctuate with their interruptions. Plato breaks with orgiastic mystery and installs a first experience based on the notion of responsibility, but there remains something of demonic mystery and thaumaturgy, as well as some of responsibility's corresponding political dimension, in Platonism as in Neoplatonism. Then comes the *mysterium tremendum* of Christian responsibility, second tremor in the genesis of responsibility as a history of secrecy, but also, as we shall see a little later, a tremor in the figures of death as figures of the gift, or in fact as gifts of death [*de la mort donnée*].

This history will never come to a close. Any history worthy of the name can neither be saturated nor closed [*se suturer*]. This history of secrecy that humans, in particular Christians, have difficulty thematizing, even more so acknowledging, is punctuated by many reversals [*renversements*] or rather conversions. Patočka uses the word "conversion" as one often does to render the ascending movement of *anabasis* by which Plato refers to the turning of one's gaze towards the Good and the intelligible sun, out of the cavern (a Good that is not yet goodness and so remains foreign to the idea of the gift). The word "conversion" is regularly rendered by words such as "turning back" (*obrácení*, 114) or "about turn" (*obrat*, 115–17). The history of secrecy, the combined history of responsibility and of the gift, has the spiral form of these turns [*tours*], intricacies [*tournures*], versions, turnings back, bends [*virages*], and conversions. One could compare it to a history of revolutions, even to history as revolution.

Taking Eugen Fink as his authority, Patočka describes the very space of Platonic speleology as the subterranean basis upon which orgiastic mystery is constructed. The cavern becomes the earth-mother from which one must finally extract oneself in order to "subordinate," as Patočka puts it, "the *orgiastic* to responsibility" (*podřídit orgiasmus zodpovědnosti*, 114). But the Platonic *anabasis* does not provide a passage from orgiastic mystery to nonmystery. It is the subordination of one mystery by another, the conversion from one secret to another. For Patočka calls the Platonic conversion that turns an eternal gaze towards the Good a "new mystery of the soul." This time the mystery becomes more internal, it takes the form of an "interior dialogue of the soul" (ibid.). Although it does correspond to a first awakening of responsibility by means of the soul's relation to the Good, this coming-to-conscience still retains its mystical element; it still takes the form of a mystery, this time unacknowledged, undeclared, denied.

One can already recognize the law for which this serves as a first example. Like those which will follow Plato's *anabasis* throughout a history of responsibility that capitalizes on secrecy, the first conversion still retains within it something of what it seems to interrupt. The logic of this conservative rupture resembles the *economy of a sacrifice* that keeps what it gives up. Sometimes it reminds one of the economy of sublation [*relève*] or *Aufhebung*, and at other times, less contradictory than it seems, of a logic of repression that still retains what is denied, surpassed, buried. Repression doesn't destroy, it displaces something from one place to another within the system. It is also a topological operation. In fact Patočka often has recourse to a type of psychoanalytic vocabulary. In the double conversion that he analyzes (that which turns away from orgiastic mystery towards Platonic or Neoplatonic mystery, as well as that which converts the latter into the Christian *mysterium tremendum*), it is true that the earlier mystery is "subordinated" (*podřazeno*) by that which follows, but it is never eliminated. In order to better describe this hierarchical subordination Patočka speaks of "incorporation" or "repression": incorporation (*přivtělení*) in the case of Platonism which retains within itself the orgiastic mystery it subordinates, subjects, and disciplines, but *repression* (*potlačení*) in the case of Christianity which retains the Platonic mystery.

This all takes place, therefore, as if conversion amounted to a process of mourning, facing up to a loss, in the sense of keeping within oneself that whose death one must endure. And what one keeps inside at the very moment that there comes into play a new experience of secrecy and a new structure of responsibility as an apportioning of mystery, is the buried memory or crypt of a more ancient secret.

To what extent should we be permitted to take literally the words *incorporation* and *repression*, such as they are encountered in the French translation of Patočka? Did he wish to give them the conceptual contours that they possess within psychoanalytic discourse, notably in a theory of mourning? Even if that is not the case, nothing prevents us from putting a psychoanalytic reading of these words to the test, at least on an experimental basis; or if not a psychoanalytic reading at least a hermeneutics that takes into account psychoanalytic concepts corresponding to the words "incorporation" and "repression," especially since our analysis concentrates on the motif of secrecy. Such a motif cannot remain immune to notions of *incorporation* (especially with respect to the work of mourning and to the figures of death that are necessarily associated with absolute secrecy) and *repression*, as the privileged process of every effect of secrecy. Historical conversions to responsibility, such as Patočka analyzes in both cases, well describe this movement by which the event of a second mystery does not destroy the first. On the contrary it keeps it inside unconsciously, after having effected a topical displacement and a hierarchical subordination: one secret is at the same time enclosed and dominated by the other. Platonic mystery thus *incorporates* orgiastic mystery and Christian mystery *represses* Platonic mystery. That, in short, is the history that would need to be "acknowledged," as if confessed! In order to avoid speaking of secrecy where Patočka speaks of mystery, one is tempted to say that secrecy, or what must be acknowledged and analyzed as historicity itself, is here the relation between these two conversions and these three mysteries (orgiastic, Platonic, and Christian). The history to be acknowledged is the secret of incorporation and repression, what occurs between one conversion and another. It concerns the time of conversion, and what is at stake in it, namely, the gift of death.

For this is not just one theme among others: a history of secrecy as history of responsibility is tied to a culture of death, in other words to the different figures of the gift of death or of putting to death [*la mort donnée*].[5] What does *donner la mort* mean in French? How does one give *oneself* death [*se donner la mort*]? How does one give it to oneself in the sense that putting oneself to death means dying while assuming responsibility for one's own death, committing suicide but also sacrificing oneself for another, *dying for the other*, thus perhaps giving one's life by giving oneself death, accepting the gift of death, such as Socrates, Christ, and others did in so many different ways. And perhaps Patočka in his own way? How does one give oneself death in that other sense in terms of which *se donner la mort* is also to interpret death, to give oneself a representation of it, a figure, a signification or destination for it? How does one give it to oneself in the sense of simply, and more generally, relating to the possibility of death (on the basis of what care, concern, or apprehension?) even if that means, following Heidegger, relating to the possibility of an impossibility? What is the relation between *se donner la mort* and sacrifice? Between putting oneself to death and dying for another? What are the relations among sacrifice, suicide, and the economy of this gift?

5. Literature concerning the secret is almost always organized around scenes and intrigues that deal with figures of death. This is something I attempt to demonstrate elsewhere, referring most often to "American" examples—"The Purloined Letter," "Bartleby the Scrivener," "The Figure in the Carpet," *The Aspern Papers*, etc.—that are the subjects of a recent seminar on the combined questions of secrecy and responsibility.

The incorporation by means of which Platonic responsibility triumphs over orgiastic mystery is the movement by which the immortality of the individual soul is affirmed—it is also the death given to Socrates, the death that he is given and that he accepts, in other words the death that he in a way gives himself when in the *Phaedo* he develops a whole discourse to give sense to his death and as it were to take the responsibility for it upon himself.

Concerning the allegory of the cave, and following Fink, Patočka has this to say:

> Plato's exposé, especially its dramatic part, is a *reversal* (*obrácení*) of traditional mysteries and of their orgiastic practices. These practices themselves tend, if not towards an alliance, at least towards a confrontation between responsibility and the orgiastic dimension. The cavern is a vestige of the subterranean place for the gathering of mysteries; it is the lap of the earth-mother. The new thinking inaugurated by Plato involves the desire to forsake the lap of the earth-mother in order to set out upon the pure "path of light," hence to completely *subordinate* (*podřídit*) the orgiastic to responsibility. That is why in Plato the path of the soul leads directly to eternity and to the source of all eternity, to the sun that is the "good."
> (114, my emphasis)

This subordination therefore takes the form of an "incorporation," whether that be understood in its psychoanalytic sense or in the wider sense of an integration that assimilates or retains within itself that which it exceeds, surpasses, or supersedes [*relève*]. The incorporation of one mystery by the other also amounts to an *incorporation* of one immortality within another, of one eternity within another. This enveloping of immortality also corresponds to a transaction between two negations or two disavowals of death. And in what amounts to a significant trait in the genealogy of responsibility, it will be marked by an internalization; by an individualization or subjectification, the soul's relation to itself as it falls back on itself in the very movement of incorporation:

Another aspect is linked with the preceding one. Platonic "conversion" makes the gaze upon the Good itself possible. This gaze is immutable, eternal like the Good. The *new mystery of the soul* that is the search for the Good occurs in the form of *an interior dialogue of the soul.* The immortality that is indissolubly linked to this dialogue thus differs from the immortality of the mysteries. It is, *for the first time in history, an immortality of the individual, since it is interior,* since it is inseparable from its own fulfillment. The Platonic doctrine of the immortality of the soul is the result of a confrontation between the orgiastic and responsibility. Responsibility triumphs over the orgiastic and *incorporates* it within itself as a *subordinated* moment, just as with Eros, who does not understand himself until he understands that he does not derive his origin from the corporeal world, from the cavern or from the shadows, but that he is uniquely a means of ascension towards the Good with its absolute demands and its rigorous *discipline.* (114, my emphasis)

Such a concept of *discipline* covers a number of senses. They all appear equally fundamental here: that of training, first of all, or exercise, the idea of the work necessary to maintain control over orgiastic mystery, to have it work in its very subordination, like a slave or servant, in other words to set to work one secret by pressing it into service for another—but also to put the demonic secret of Eros to work within this new hierarchy. Secondly, this discipline is also philosophy, or the dialectic, to the extent that it can be taught, precisely as a discipline, at the same time exoteric and esoteric; as well as that of the exercise that consists in learning to die in order to attain the new immortality, that is, *meletē thanatou,* the care taken with death, the exercise of death, the "practicing (for) death" that Socrates speaks of in the *Phaedo.*

The *Phaedo* explicitly names philosophy: it is the attentive anticipation of death, the care brought to bear upon dying, the meditation on the best way to receive, give, or give oneself death, the experience of a *vigil* over the possibility of death, and over the possibility of death as impossibility. That very idea, namely, this *meletē* or *epimeleia* that one can rightly translate by "care" or "solicitude," opens the vein—and begins the vigil—within which will be inscribed the *Sorge* ("care") in the sense Heidegger confers on it in *Being and Time.*[6] In particular let us think of the moment when Heidegger, following the tradition of the *cura* but without naming Plato, evokes nothing more than the *solicitudo* of the Vulgate, Seneca, and the *merimna* of the Stoics (§42, 199 [243]), which, however, *like* the Platonic *meletē,* also signifies care, concern, and solicitude.

The famous passage of the *Phaedo* (80e) that Patočka obliquely refers to but neither analyzes nor even cites, describes a sort of subjectivizing interiorization, the movement of the soul's gathering of itself, a fleeing of the body towards its interior where it withdraws into itself in order to recall itself to itself, in order to be next to itself, in order to keep itself in this gesture of re*member*ing. This conversion turns the soul around and amasses it upon itself. It is such a movement of gathering, as in the prefix *syn,* that announces the coming-to-conscience, as well as that representative conscience of the self by which the secret, but this time in the sense of the Latin *secretum* (from *secernere*), separate, distinct, discerned, could be kept as an objective representation. For one of the threads we are following here is this history of secrecy and of its differentiated semantics, from the Greek sense of the mystical and cryptic to the Latin *secretum* and the German *Geheimnis.*

Socrates recalls a certain invisibility of the *psyché,* after having played again on *aïdēs-haidēs,* as he does in the *Cratylus,* on the fact that the invisible soul (*aides* also meaning "one who doesn't see," "blind") goes to its death in an invisible place that is also Hades (*Haidēs*), this invisibility of the *aïdēs* being in itself a figure of secrecy:

> The truth rather is that the soul which is pure at departing
> and draws after her no bodily taint [in other words Socra-

6. Martin Heidegger, *Being and Time,* trans. John Macquarrie and Edward Robinson (New York: Harper and Row, 1962). Page numbers from this edition appear in brackets following paragraph and page numbers from the later German editions.—Trans. note.

tes describes this separation of the invisible soul, this se-
creting of the self by means of which the soul retreats
from the visible body to assemble itself within itself, in
order to be next to itself within its interior invisibility—
separation and invisibility indeed being the criteria for
secrecy], having never voluntarily during life had connex-
ion with the body (*ouden koinōnousa autō en tō biō hekousa
einai*), which she is ever avoiding (*pheugousa*), herself gath-
ered in herself (*synethroismenē hautēs eis heautēn*) [whenever
Levinas refers to the *Phaedo*, as he often does in his different texts on death, he underlines this assembling of the
soul upon itself as the moment when the self identifies
with itself in its relation to death], and making such ab-
straction her perpetual study (*hate meletōsa aei touto*)—all
this means that she has been a true disciple of philosophy
(*he orthōs philosophousa*); and therefore has in fact been always practising how to die without complaint (*kai tō onti
tethnanai meletōsa rhadiōs*). For is not such a life the practice
of death (*ē ou tout' an eie meletē thanatou*)?[7]

This canonical passage is one of the most often cited, or at least
evoked, in the history of philosophy. It is rarely subjected to a
close reading. One might be surprised to learn that Heidegger
doesn't quote it, in any case not once in *Being and Time*, not even
in the passages devoted to care or to the being-towards-death. For
it is indeed a matter of care, a "keeping-vigil-for," a solicitude for
death that constitutes the relation to self of that which, in existence, relates to oneself. For one never reinforces enough the fact
that it is not the *psychē* that is there in the first place and that comes
thereafter to be concerned about its death, to keep watch over it,
to be the very vigil of its death. No, the soul only distinguishes
itself, separates itself, and assembles within itself in the experience
of this *meletē tou thanatou*. It is nothing other than this concern for
dying as a relation to self and an assembling of self. It only returns
to itself, in both senses of assembling itself and waking itself, be-

7. *The Dialogues of Plato*, vol. 1, ed. and trans. B. Jowett, 4th edition (Oxford:
Clarendon Press, 1953), 435.

coming conscious [*s'éveiller*], in the sense of consciousness of self in general, through this concern for death. And Patočka is quite right to speak here of mystery or secrecy in the constitution of a *psychē* or of an individual and responsible self. For it is thus that the soul separates itself in recalling itself to itself, and so it becomes individualized, interiorized, becomes its very invisibility. And hence it philosophizes from the beginning. Philosophy isn't something that comes to the soul by accident, for it is nothing other than this vigil over death that watches out for death and watches over death, as if over the very life of the soul. The psyche as life, as breath of life, as *pneuma*, only appears out of this concerned anticipation of dying. The anticipation of this vigil already resembles a provisional mourning, a vigil [*veille*] as wake [*veillée*].

But this vigil that marks the event of a new secret incorporates within its discipline the orgiastic secret that it subordinates and renders dormant. Because of this *incorporation* that envelops demonic or orgiastic mystery, philosophy remains a sort of thaumaturgy even as it accedes to responsibility:

> In Neoplatonism this conception results in making the demonic into a subjugated realm (Eros is a great demon) [Eros is thus subjugated but not annihilated] within the perspective of the true philosopher who has overcome all its temptations. Whence a consequence that might surprise us: the philosopher is also a great thaumaturge. The Platonic philosopher is a magician [think of Socrates and his demon], namely, Faust. Gilles Quispel, a Dutch historian of ideas [Patočka regularly refers, in his text, to the latter's book *Gnosis als Weltreligion*], sees in this one of the principal origins of the Faust legend and of Faustism in general, in terms of those "infinite aspirations" that make Faust so dangerous but which also, finally, represent a possible means of salvation. (114–15)

This concern for death, this awakening that keeps vigil over death, this conscience that looks death in the face is another name for freedom. There again, without wanting to neglect the essential differences, we can see in this link between the concern of the being-towards-death, accepted in and of itself (*eigentlich*), and freedom, that is, responsibility, a structure analogous to that of the *Dasein* as described by Heidegger. Patočka is never far from Heidegger, in particular when he continues as follows:

> Another important moment: the Platonic philosopher triumphs over death in the sense that he doesn't run from it, he looks it straight in the face. His philosophy is *meletē thanatou*, concern for death; the concern of the soul is inseparable from the concern for death which becomes authentic concern (*pravá*) for life; (eternal) life is born from this event of looking death in the face, from the triumph (*přemožení*) over death (*perhaps it is nothing but this "triumph"*). Yet when that is combined with the relation to the Good, with the identification with the Good and with deliverance from the demonic and the orgiastic, it signifies *the reign of responsibility and, along with it, of freedom*. The soul is absolutely free, it chooses its own destiny. (115, my emphasis)

What is the significance of this allusion to the fact that "the reign of responsibility and, along with it, of freedom" consists perhaps of a triumph over death, in other words of a triumph of life (*The Triumph of Life* Shelley would have called it, inverting the traditional figure of all the triumphs over death)? Patočka even suggests in a parenthesis that all of that—so-called eternal life, responsibility, freedom—*is perhaps nothing other than* this triumph. Now a triumph retains traces of a struggle. It is as if a victory has been won in the course of a war between two fundamentally inseparable adversaries; the news rings out a day later at the time of the feast that commemorates (another wake) and preserves the memory of the war—this *polemos* that Patočka speaks of so often and grants so much importance in these *Heretical Essays*. The essay on "The Wars of the Twentieth Century and the Twentieth Century as War" (129–46) is one of those that Ricoeur, in his preface to the French edition, judges "strange and in many respects frightening" (8). It involves a paradoxical phenomenology of darkness but also a secret alliance between night and day. Such a joining of opposites plays an essential role in Patočka's political thought, and although he cites only Ernst Jünger (*Der Arbeiter* and *Der Kampf als inneres Erlebnis*) and Teilhard de Chardin (*Writings in the Time of War*), his discourse is at times close to Heidegger's very compli- cated and equivocal discussion of the Heraclitean *polemos*, closer to it than ever and, it seems to me, more so than Ricoeur says in his preface, in spite of one essential difference that can't be elaborated upon here.[8]

War is a further experience of the gift of death [*la mort donnée*] (I put my enemy to death and I give my own life in sacrificing myself "for my country"). Patočka interprets the Heraclitean *po- lemos* in this way: rather than being an "expansion of 'life'," it represents the prevalence of Darkness, the "desire for the freedom of risk in the *aristeia*, that excellence at the extreme limit of human possibility that the best of us choose once they decide to exchange the short-lived prolongation of a comfortable life for a durable fame in the memory of mortals" (146). This *polemos* unites adversaries, it brings together those who are opposed (Heidegger often insisted on the same thing). The *front*, as the site upon which the First World War was waged, provides a historic figure for this *polemos* that brings enemies together as though they were conjoined in the extreme proximity of the face-to-face. This exceptional and troubling glorification of the front perhaps presages another type of mourning, namely, the loss of this front during and especially after the Second World War, the disappearance of this confronta- tion which allowed one to identify the enemy and even and espe- cially to *identify with* the enemy. After the Second World War, as Patočka might say in the manner of Carl Schmitt, one loses the image or face of the enemy, one loses the war and perhaps, from then on, the very possibility of politics. This identification *of* the

8. I deal with this question in "Heidegger's Ear: Philopolemology (*Geschlecht* IV)," in John Sallis, ed., *Reading Heidegger: Commemorations* (Bloomington: Indiana University Press, 1993).

enemy, which, in the experience of the front, remains always very close to an identification *with* the enemy, is what troubles and fascinates Patočka more than anything else.

> The same sentiment and vision are there for Teilhard de Chardin when he makes the front the experience of the superhuman and of the divine. Jünger says at some point that as they attack the opposing troops become two parts of a single force, melding into a single body, and he adds: "A single body—what a strange comparison. Whoever understands that assumes his own value as well as that of the enemy, he lives at the same time in the whole and in the parts. Such a person can then imagine himself to be a divinity who is dangling these variegated threads from his fingers . . . with a smile on his lips." Is it by chance that two thinkers, so profoundly different from one another, but having such an intimate experience of the front, both arrive from different perspectives at comparisons that return to the Heraclitean vision of being as *polemos?* In fact doesn't one find there something of the irreducible sense of the history of Western humanity, an aspect of the sense that today becomes the sense of human history in general? (146)

But if it commemorates death and victory over death, this triumph also marks the moment of celebration when the survivor who is forced to mourn experiences the joy of survival or "superexistence" [*sur-vie*] in an almost maniacal way, as Freud pointed out. In this genealogy of responsibility and of freedom, of their "reign" as Patočka calls it, the triumphant affirmation of the free and responsible self on the part of a mortal or finite being can indeed be expressed maniacally. Thus, in the same disavowal, it would hide, from others or from itself, more than one secret: that of the orgiastic mystery that it has enslaved, subordinated, and incorporated, and that of its own mortality that it refuses or denies in the very experience of its triumph.

Such a genealogy thus seems indeed ambiguous. The interpretation of such a philosophical or philosophico-political emergence of absolute freedom ("the soul is absolutely free, it chooses its own destiny" [115]) seems nothing other than straightforward and self-sufficient; but it betrays a disquieting assessment of things. For in spite of the implicit praise for the responsible freedom that awakes from its orgiastic or demonic sleep, Patočka recognizes in this vigilance a "new mythology." Although it is incorporated, disciplined, subjugated, and enslaved, the orgiastic is not annihilated. It continues to motivate subterraneously a mythology of responsible freedom that is at the same time a politics, indeed the still partly intact foundation of politics in the West; it continues to motivate such a freedom after the second turnaround or conversion that is Christianity:

> Thus there is born a new and shining mythology of the soul, founded on the duality of the *authentic* (*pravé*) and responsible on the one hand, and of the extraordinary and orgiastic on the other. The orgiastic *is not eliminated but disciplined, enslaved* (*není odstraněno, ale zkázněno a učiněno služebným*). (115, my emphasis)

One can recognize the proximity to Heidegger throughout Patočka's discourse, both here and elsewhere, but the differences between them, whether explicit or potential, are nonetheless significant. The theme of authenticity, the links among care, being-towards-death, freedom, and responsibility, the very idea of a genesis or a history of egological subjectivity, all such ideas certainly have a Heideggerian flavor to them. But this genealogy is hardly Heideggerian in style when it takes into account an incorporation of an earlier mystery that blurs the limits of every epoch. Without wanting to assign Patočka a particular heritage at all costs, one might say that certain of his genealogist tendencies seem at times more Nietzschean than Husserlian or Heideggerian. Moreover, Patočka cites Nietzsche, for whom Christianity was the Platonism of the people (116). Such an idea is "correct," he notes, up to a certain point, the difference, which is not negligible, being rather *nothing* itself, residing in the horrifying thinking of the abyss one encounters in Nietzsche.

If the orgiastic remains enveloped, if the demonic persists, in-

corporated and dominated, in a new experience of responsible freedom, then the latter never becomes what it is. It will never become
pure and authentic, or absolutely new. The Platonic philosopher
is in no better a position than an animal to "look at" death in the
face and so assume that authenticity of existence linked to the
epimeleia tēs psykhēs as *meletē thanatou*, the concerned caring for the
soul that is a concern that keeps watch for/over death. And it is
through that very possibility that the doubling of secrecy or mystery blurs whatever limits form the major outlines of Heidegger's
existential critique. There is first of all demonic mystery in itself,
one might say. Then there is the structure of secrecy that keeps
that mystery hidden, incorporated, concealed but alive, in the
structure of free responsibility that claims to go beyond it and that
in fact only succeeds by subordinating mystery and keeping it
subjugated. The secret of responsibility would consist of keeping
secret, or "incorporated," the secret of the demonic and thus of
preserving within itself a nucleus of irresponsibility or of absolute
unconsciousness, something Patočka will later call "orgiastic irresponsibility" (121).

In hypothesizing the moment that Patočka identifies as that of
the Platonic philosopher, we could perhaps recover the semantic
difference between mystery and what should more strictly be
called secrecy, the *secretum* whose sense points towards a separation
(*se-cernere*) and more generally towards the objective representation
that the conscious subject keeps within itself: what it knows, what
it knows how to represent, even though it cannot or will not de-
clare or avow that representation. The *secretum* supposes the constitution of this liberty of the soul as the conscience of a responsible
subject. In short, waking from demonic *mystery*, surpassing the
demonic, involves attaining the possibility of the *secretum*, of the
keeping of a secret. For it also involves gaining access to the individualization of the relation to oneself, to the ego that separates
itself from the community of fusion. But this simply means ex-
changing one secret for another. A particular economy would hap-
pily sacrifice mystery for secrecy within a history of truth as a
history of dissimulation, within a genealogy that is a cryptology
or general *mystology*.

All that derives therefore from a mythomorphic or mythopoetic *incorporation*. In formalizing and in rigidifying a little what Patočka says, without for all that, I hope, betraying it, I would hold that, in the first place, he simply describes the Platonic incorporation of demonic mystery and orgiastic irresponsibility. But can one not go further and say that this incorporation is in turn *repressed* by a certain Christianity, in the precise moment Patočka calls the Christian *reversal?* One would thus be tempted to distinguish two economies, or one economy with two systems: *incorporation* and *repression.*

The essentially political dimension of this crypto- or mysto-genealogy becomes clearer. It seems to describe what is at stake in the passage from Platonic secrecy to the Christian secret of the *mysterium tremendum*. In order to examine this it will be necessary to distinguish three important motifs in this genealogy that combines secrecy with responsibility.

1. One must never forget, and precisely for political reasons, that the mystery that is incorporated, then repressed, is never destroyed. This genealogy has an axiom, namely, that history never effaces what it buries; it always keeps within itself the secret of whatever it encrypts, the secret of its secret. This is a secret history of kept secrets. For that reason the genealogy is also an economy. Orgiastic mystery recurs indefinitely, it is always at work: not only in Platonism, as we have seen, but also in Christianity and even in the space of the *Aufklärung* and of secularization in general. Patočka encourages us to learn a political lesson from this, one for today and tomorrow, by reminding us that every revolution, whether atheistic or religious, bears witness to a return of the sacred in the form of an enthusiasm or fervor, otherwise known as the presence of the gods within us. Speaking of this "new rise of the orgiastic floodwaters," something that remains forever imminent and that corresponds to an abdication of responsibility, Patočka gives the example of the religious fervor that took hold during the French Revolution. Given the affinity between the sacred and secrecy, and the practice of sacrifice in initiation ceremonies, it might be said that all revolutionary fervor produces its slogans as though they were sacrificial rites or effects of secrecy.

21

Patočka doesn't say as much explicitly but his quotation from Durkheim seems to point in that direction:

> The aptitude of society for setting itself up as a god or for creating gods was never more apparent than during the first years of the French Revolution. At that time, in fact, under the influence of the general enthusiasm, things purely laical by nature were transformed by public opinion into sacred things: these were the Fatherland, Liberty, Reason.

And after this quote from *The Elementary Forms of the Religious Life*,[9] Patočka continues:

> This is of course an enthusiasm that, in spite of the cult of reason, retains its orgiastic character, one which is undisciplined or insufficiently disciplined by the personal relation to responsibility. The danger of a new fall into the orgiastic is imminent. (121)

Such a warning does no more than oppose one form of mourning to another (such are the paradoxes or aporias of every economy), melancholy to triumph or triumph to melancholy, one form of depression to another form of depression, or, and this amounts to the same thing, one form of depression to a form of resistance to depression. One escapes the demonic orgiastic by means of the Platonic triumph, and one escapes the latter by means of the sacrifice or repentance of the Christian "reversal," that is, by means of the Christian "repression."

2. If I am not exaggerating by relating this interpretation of the *epimeleia tēs psykhēs* to a psychoanalytic economy of secrecy as mourning or of mourning as secrecy, I might say that what separates that economy from Heidegger's influence is its essential Christianity. Heideggerian thought was not simply a constant attempt to separate itself from Christianity (a gesture that always

9. Emile Durkheim, *The Elementary Forms of the Religious Life*, trans. Joseph Ward Swain (New York: The Free Press, 1965), 244-45.

needs to be related—however complex this relation—to the incredible unleashing of anti-Christian violence represented by Nazism's most official and explicit ideology, something one tends to forget these days). The same Heideggerian thinking often consists, notably in *Sein und Zeit*, in repeating on an ontological level Christian themes and texts that have been "de-Christianized." Such themes and texts are then presented as ontic, anthropological, or contrived attempts that come to a sudden halt on the way to an ontological recovery of their own originary possibility (whether that be, for example, the *status corruptionis*, the difference between the authentic and inauthentic or the fall (*Verfallen*) into the *One*, whether it be the *sollicitudo* and care, the pleasure of seeing and of curiosity, of the authentic or vulgar concept of time, of the texts of the Vulgate, of Saint Augustine or of Kierkegaard). Patočka makes an inverse yet symmetrical gesture, which therefore amounts to the same thing. He reontologizes the historic themes of Christianity and attributes to revelation or to the *mysterium tremendum* the ontological content that Heidegger attempts to remove from it.

3. But Patočka does not do this in order to redirect things along the path of an orthodox Christianity. His own heresy intersects with what one might call, a little provocatively, that other heresy, namely, the twisting or diverting by which the Heideggerian repetition, in its one way, affects Christianity.

On two or three occasions Patočka denounces the persistence of a type of Platonism—and of a type of Platonic politics—at the heart of European Christianity. For, in short, the latter has not sufficiently repressed Platonism in the course of its reversal, and it still mouths its words. In this sense, and from the political point of view, Nietzsche's idea of Christianity as the Platonism of the people would once more be reinforced (found, up to a certain point, to be "correct," as we were saying just now).

A. *On the one hand*, for Patočka responsible decision-making is subjected to knowledge:

> While all the time condemning the Platonic solution, Christian theology adopts important elements of it [it con-

demns the orgiastic, certainly, but on the basis of a meta-physics of knowledge as *sophia tou kosmou:* knowledge of the order of the world and subordination of ethics and politics to objective knowledge]. Platonic rationalism, the Platonic desire to subordinate responsibility itself to the objectivity of knowledge, continues to secretly influence (*v podzemí*) Christian conceptions. Theology itself rests on a "natural" foundation, the "supernatural" being under-stood as a fulfilling of the natural. (119)

To "subordinate responsibility to the objectivity of knowledge," is obviously, in Patočka's view, to discount responsibility. And how can we not subscribe to this implication? Saying that a responsible decision must be taken on the basis of knowledge seems to define the condition of possibility of responsibility (one can't make a responsible decision without science or conscience, without knowing what one is doing, for what reasons, in view of what and under what conditions), at the same time as it defines the condition of impossibility of this same responsibility (if decision-making is relegated to a knowledge that it is content to follow or to develop, then it is no more a responsible decision, it is the technical deploy-ment of a cognitive apparatus, the simple mechanistic deployment of a theorem). This *aporia of responsibility* would thus define the relation between the Platonic and Christian paradigms throughout the history of morality and politics.

B. That is why, *on the other hand*, although Patočka inscribes his ethical or legal, and in particular his political discourse, within the perspective of a Christian eschatology, he manages to outline something of what remains "unthought" in Christianity. Whether ethical or political, the Christian consciousness of responsibility is incapable of reflecting on the Platonic thinking that it represses, and at the same time it is incapable of reflecting on the orgiastic mystery that Platonic thinking incorporates. That appears in the definition of that which is precisely the place and subject of all responsibility, namely, the *person*. Immediately after describing the Christian "reversal" or "repression" in the *mysterium tremendum*, Patočka writes:

> In the final analysis the soul [in the Christian mystery] is
> not a relation to an *object*, however elevated (such as the
> Platonic Good) [which implies, therefore, "such as in Pla-
> tonism where the soul is the relation to a transcendent
> Good that also governs the ideal order of the Greek *polis*
> or the Roman *civitas*"], but to a person who fixes it in his
> gaze while at the same time remaining beyond the reach of
> the gaze of that soul. As for knowing what this person is,
> such a question has not yet received an adequate thematic
> development within the perspective of Christianity. (116)

The inadequacy of this thematization comes to rest on the
threshold of responsibility. It doesn't thematize what a responsible
person *is*, that is, what he *must be*, namely, this exposing of the
soul to the gaze of another person, of a person as transcendent
other, as an other who looks at me, but who looks without the-
subject-who-says-I being able to reach that other, see her, hold
her within the reach of my gaze. And let us not forget that an
inadequate thematization of what responsibility is or *must be* is
also an *irresponsible* thematization: not knowing, having neither a
sufficient knowledge or consciousness of what being *responsible*
means, is of itself a lack of responsibility. In order to be responsible
it is necessary to respond to or answer to what being responsible
means. For if it is true that the concept of responsibility has, in
the most reliable continuity of its history, always implied involvement in action, doing, a *praxis*, a *decision* that exceeds simple conscience or simple theoretical understanding, it is also true that the
same concept requires a decision or responsible action to answer
for itself *consciously*, that is, with knowledge of a thematics of what
is done, of what action signifies, its causes, ends, etc. In debates
concerning responsibility one must always take into account this
original and irreducible complexity that links theoretical consciousness (which must also be a thetic or thematic consciousness) to
"practical" conscience (ethical, legal, political), if only to avoid the
arrogance of so many "clean consciences." We must continually
remind ourselves that some part of irresponsibility insinuates itself
wherever one demands responsibility without sufficiently concep-

tualizing and thematizing what "responsibility" means; *that is to say everywhere*. One can say *everywhere* a priori and nonempirically, for if the complex linkage between the theoretical and practical that we just referred to is, quite clearly, irreducible, then the heterogeneity between the two linked orders is just as irreducible. Hence, the activating of responsibility (decision, act, *praxis*) will always take place before and beyond any theoretical or thematic determination. It will have to decide without it, independently from knowledge; that will be the condition of a practical idea of freedom. We should therefore conclude that not only is the thematization of the concept of responsibility always inadequate but that it is always so because it must be so. And what goes here for responsibility also goes, for the same reasons, for freedom and for decision.

The heterogeneity that we have identified between the exercise of responsibility and its theoretical or even doctrinal thematization, is also, surely, what ties responsibility to *heresy*, to the *hairesis* as choice, election, preference, inclination, bias, that is, decision; but also as a school (philosophical, religious, literary) that corresponds to that bias; and finally heresy in the sense fixed in the vocabulary of the Catholic Church and made more general since, namely, departure from a doctrine, difference within and difference from the officially and publicly stated doctrine and the institutional community that is governed by it. Now, to the extent that this heresy always marks a difference or departure, keeping itself apart from what is publicly or commonly declared, it isn't only, in its very possibility, the essential condition of responsibility; paradoxically, it also destines responsibility to the resistance or dissidence of a type of secrecy. It keeps responsibility apart [*tient la responsabilité à l'écart*] and in secret. And responsibility *insists on* what is apart [tient à *l'écart*] and secret.

Dissidence, difference, heresy, resistance, secrecy—so many experiences that are paradoxical in the strong sense that Kierkegaard gives to the word. In fact it comes down to linking secrecy to a responsibility that consists, according to the most convincing and convinced *doxa*, in *responding*, hence in answering to the other, before the other and before the law, and if possible publicly, answering for itself, its intentions, its aims, and for the name of the agent deemed responsible. This relation between responsibility and responding is not common to all languages but it does exist in Czech (*odpovědnost*).

What I have said might seem faithful to the spirit of Patočka's heresy at the same time as it is heretical with respect to that very heresy. The paradox can in fact be interpreted directly from what Patočka maintains concerning the person and concerning the Christian *mysterium tremendum;* but also against it, in that when he speaks of an inadequate thematization he seems to appeal to some ultimate adequacy of thematization that could be accomplished. On the other hand, the theme of thematization, the sometimes phenomenological motif of thematic conscience, is the thing that is, if not denied, at least strictly limited in its pertinence by that other more radical form of responsibility that exposes me dissymmetrically to the gaze of the other; where my gaze, precisely as regards me [*ce qui me regarde*], is no longer the measure of all things. The concept of responsibility is one of those strange concepts that give food for thought without giving themselves over to thematization. It presents itself neither as a theme nor as a thesis, it gives without being seen [*sans se donner à voir*], without presenting itself in person by means of a "fact of being seen" that can be phenomenologically intuited. This paradoxical concept also has the structure of a type of secret—what is called, in the code of certain religious practices, mystery. The exercise of responsibility seems to leave no choice but this one, however uncomfortable it may be, of paradox, heresy, and secrecy. More serious still, it must always run the risk of conversion and apostasy: there is no responsibility without a dissident and inventive rupture with respect to tradition, authority, orthodoxy, rule, or doctrine.

The dissymmetry of the gaze, this disproportion that relates me, and whatever concerns me, to a gaze that I don't see and that remains secret from me although it commands me, is, according to Patočka, what is identified in Christian mystery as the frightening, terrifying mystery, the *mysterium tremendum*. Such a terror has no place in the transcendent experience that relates Platonic responsibility to the *agathon*. Nor does it have any place in the politics that is so instituted. But the terror of this secret exceeds and precedes the complacent relation of a subject to an object.

Is the reference to this abyssal dissymmetry that occurs when one is exposed to the gaze of the other a motif that derives firstly and uniquely from Christianity, even if it be from an inadequately thematized Christianity? Let us leave aside the question of whether one finds something that at least represents its equivalent "before" or "after" the Gospels, in Judaism or in Islam. If we restrict ourselves to reading what Patočka writes, we have no doubt that in his view Christianity—and the Christian Europe that he never dissociates from it—remains the most powerful means of plumbing the depths of this abyss of responsibility, even if it is limited by the weight of what remains unthought, in particular its incorrigible Platonism:

> Because of its foundation (*základ*) within the abyssal profundity of the soul, Christianity represents to this day the most powerful means—never yet superseded but not yet thought right through either—by which man is able to struggle against his own decline. (117)

One should understand that in saying that Christianity has not been thought right through Patočka intends that such a task be undertaken; not only by means of a more thorough thematization but also by means of a political and historical setting-in-train, by means of political and historical action; and he advocates that according to the logic of a messianic eschatology that is nevertheless indissociable from phenomenology. Something has not yet arrived, neither at Christianity nor by means of Christianity. What has not yet arrived at or happened to Christianity is Christianity. Christianity has not yet come to Christianity. What has not yet come about is the fulfillment, within history and in political history, and first and foremost in European politics, of the new responsibility announced by the *mysterium tremendum*. There has not yet been an authentically Christian politics because there remains this residue of the Platonic *polis*. Christian politics must break more definitively and more radically with Greco-Roman Platonic politics in order to finally fulfill the *mysterium tremendum*. Only on this condition will Europe have a future, and will there be a future in general, for Patočka speaks less of a past event or fact than he does of a promise. The promise has already been made. The time of such a promise defines both the experience of the *mysterium tremendum* and the double repression that institutes it, the *double repression* by means of which it represses but retains within itself *both* the orgiastic incorporated by Platonism *and* Platonism itself.

What is implicit yet explosive in Patočka's text can be extended in a radical way, for it is heretical with respect to a certain Christianity and a certain Heideggerianism but also with respect to all the important European discourses. Taken to its extreme, the text seems to suggest on the one hand that Europe will not be what it must be until it becomes fully Christian, until the *mysterium tremendum* is adequately thematized. On the other hand it also suggests that the Europe to come will no longer be Greek, Greco-Roman, or even Roman. The most radical insistence of the *mysterium tremendum* would be upon a Europe so new (or so old) that it would be freed from the Greek or Roman memory that is so commonly invoked in speaking of it; freed to the extent of breaking all ties with this memory, becoming heterogeneous to it. What would be the secret of a Europe emancipated from both Athens and Rome?

In the first place there is the enigma of an impossible and inevitable transition, that from Platonism to Christianity. We should not be surprised to notice that in the moment of the reversal or repression a privileged status is accorded the unstable, multiple, and somewhat spectral historic figure (one that becomes all the more fascinating and exciting) that is called Neoplatonism, and notably whatever relates this Neoplatonism to the political power of Rome. But Patočka not only refers to the political profile of Neoplatonism; he also makes oblique reference to something that is not a thing but that is probably the very site of the most decisive paradox, namely, the *gift that is not a present*, the gift of something that remains inaccessible, unpresentable, and as a consequence secret. The event of this gift would link the essence without essence of the gift to secrecy. For one might say that a gift that could be recognized as such in the light of day, a gift destined for recognition, would immediately annul itself. The gift is the secret itself, if the secret *itself* can be told. Secrecy is the last word of the gift which is the last word of the secret.

Discussion concerning the passage from Plato to Christianity immediately follows the allusion to the "shining new mythology of the soul, founded on the duality of the authentic and the responsible on the one hand, and the extraordinary and orgiastic on the other." As Patočka then states, "the orgiastic is not eliminated but disciplined, dominated."

> This theme takes on capital importance when, with the end of the *polis-civitas*, the Roman principality presents the problem of a new responsibility, founded upon transcendence in the social context as well, a responsibility towards a State that can no longer be a community of persons who are equal in respect of their freedom. From then on freedom is determined not by relations among equals (compatriots) but by a relation to the transcendent Good. That poses new questions and makes possible new solutions. In the final analysis the social problem of the Roman Empire is also consolidated on grounds made possible by the Platonic conception of the soul.
>
> The Neoplatonist philosopher Julian the Apostate sitting on the imperial throne represents—as Quispel made clear—an important episode in the relations between the orgiastic and the discipline of responsibility. Christianity has not been able to surpass this Platonic solution except by *yet another reversal*. Responsible life itself was conceived in that event as the *gift* of something that, in the end, while having the characteristics of the Good, also presented the traits of something *inaccessible* (*nepřístupného*) to which man is forever enslaved—the traits of a mystery that has the last word. Christianity understands the good in a different way from Plato, as goodness that is forgetful of itself and as love (in no way orgiastic) that denies itself. (115, my emphasis)

Let us emphasize the word "gift." Between on the one hand this denial that involves renouncing the self, this abnegation of the gift, of goodness, or of the generosity of the gift that must withdraw, hide, in fact sacrifice itself in order to give, and on the other hand the repression that would transform the gift into an economy of sacrifice, is there not a secret affinity, an unavoidable risk of contamination of two possibilities as close one to the other as they are different from each other? For what is given in this trembling, in the actual trembling of terror, is nothing other than death itself, a new significance for death, a new apprehension of death, a new way in which to give oneself death or to put oneself to death [*se donner la mort*]. The difference between Platonism and Christianity would be above all "a reversal in the face of death and of eternal death, living in anguish and hope that couldn't be more closely allied one with the other, trembling in the consciousness of sin and offering one's whole being in the sacrifice of repentance" (117). Such is the rupture that functions in the mode of, and within the limits of, a repression: between the metaphysics, ethics, and politics of the Platonic Good (that is, the "incorporated" orgiastic mystery) and the *mysterium tremendum* of Christian responsibility:

> No more the orgiastic, which remains not only subordinated but, in certain extreme cases, completely repressed; instead, a *mysterium tremendum*. *Tremendum*, because responsibility resides henceforth not in an essence that is accessible to the human gaze, that of the Good and the One, but in the relation to a supreme, absolute and inaccessible being that holds us in check not by exterior but interior force. (116)

Since he knows Heidegger's ideas and language so well, Patočka's allusion is made with quite conscious intent. He speaks of a supreme being, of God as one who, holding me from within and within his gaze, defines everything regarding me, and so rouses me to responsibility. The definition of God as supreme being is the onto-theological proposition that Heidegger rejects when he speaks of the originary and essential responsibility of the *Dasein*. Within the hearing of this call (*Ruf*) on the basis of which it is experienced as originally responsible, guilty (*schuldig*), or indebted before any fault in particular and before any determined debt, the

Dasein is in the first place not responsible to any determined being who looks at it or speaks to it. When Heidegger describes what he names the call or the sense of calling (*Rufsinn*) as experience of care and original phenomenon of the *Dasein* in its originary being-responsible or being-guilty (*Schuldigsein*), the existential analysis that he is proposing claims to go beyond any theological perspective (§54, 269 [313]). This originarity does not imply any relation of the *Dasein* to a supreme being as origin of the voice that speaks to the *Gewissen*, or conscience, or as origin of the gaze before which moral conscience must stand; in fact it excludes such a relation. On several occasions Heidegger describes the Kantian representation of the tribunal *before* which or *in whose sight* conscience must appear as an image (*Bild*), thereby disqualifying it at least from an ontological point of view (§55, 271 [316]; §59, 293 [339]). On the other hand the silent voice that calls the *Dasein* is immune from all possible identification. It is absolutely indeterminate, even if "the peculiar indefiniteness of the caller and the impossibility of making more definite what this caller is, are not just nothing" ("*Die eigentümliche Unbestimmtheit und Unbestimmbarkeit des Rufers ist nicht nichts*") (§57, 275 [319]). The origin of responsibility does not in any way reduce, originarily, to a supreme being. But there is no mystery in that. Nor any secret. There is no mystery to this indetermination and indeterminacy. The fact that the voice remains silent and is not the voice of anyone in particular, of any determinable identity, is the condition of the *Gewissen* (that which is translated loosely as moral conscience—let us call it the responsible conscience), but that in no way implies that this voice is a secret or "mysterious voice" ("*geheimnisvolle Stimme*") (§56, 274 [318]).

Thus Patočka deliberately takes an opposite tack to Heidegger. He is no doubt convinced that there is no true binding responsibility or obligation that doesn't come from someone, from a person such as an absolute being who transfixes me, takes possession of me, holds me in its hand and in its gaze (even though through this dissymmetry I don't see it; it is essential that I don't see it). This supreme being, this infinite other, first comes across me, it falls upon me (it is true that Heidegger also says that the call whose source remains indeterminable comes from me while falling upon me, it comes out of me as it comes across me—"*Der Ruf kommt aus mir und doch über mich*" [§57, 275 (320)]). While seeming to contradict Heidegger by assigning the origin of my responsibility to a supreme being, Patočka also seems to contradict himself, for he says elsewhere that Nietzsche was quite correct in describing Christianity as the Platonism of the people because "the Christian God reinforces the onto-theological conception of transcendence as something evident," whereas on the other hand there is "a profound difference of principle" between Christianity and onto-theology. In order to escape this contradiction he will need to keep his reference to a supreme being distinct from all onto-theological meaning in the sense that Heidegger, and Heidegger alone, gave to it and whose concept he sought to legitimize. This is without doubt an implicit project of Patočka's discourse.

The crypto- or mysto-genealogy of responsibility is woven with the double and inextricably intertwined thread of the gift and of death: in short of the *gift of death*. The gift made to me by God as he holds me in his gaze and in his hand while remaining inaccessible to me, the terribly dissymmetrical gift of the *mysterium tremendum* only allows me to respond and only rouses me to the responsibility it gives me by making a gift of death [*en me donnant la mort*], giving the secret of death, a new experience of death.

The question of whether this discourse on the gift and on the gift of death is or is not a discourse on sacrifice and on *dying for the other* is something that we must now analyze. Especially since this investigation into the secret of responsibility is eminently historical and political. It concerns the very essence or future of European politics.

Like the *polis* and the Grecian politics that corresponds to it, the Platonic moment incorporates demonic mystery in vain; it introduces or *presents* itself as a moment without mystery. What distinguishes the moment of the Platonic *polis both from* the orgiastic mystery that it incorporates *and* from the Christian *mysterium tremendum* that represses it, is the fact that in the first case one openly declares that secrecy will not be allowed. There is a place for secrecy, for the *mysterium* or for the mystical in what *precedes* or what *follows* Platonism (demonic orgiastic mystery or the *mysterium tremendum*); but according to Patočka there is none such in the philosophy and politics of the Platonic tradition. Politics excludes the mystical. Thenceforth whatever there is in Europe and even in modern Europe that inherits this politics of Greco-Platonic provenance, either neglects, represses, or excludes from itself every essential possibility of secrecy and every link between responsibility and the keeping of a secret; everything that allows responsibility to be dedicated to secrecy. From there it takes very little to envisage an inevitable passage from the *democratic* to the *totalitarian;* it is the simple process that takes place by opening such a passage. The consequences will be most serious; they deserve a second look.

TWO

Beyond: Giving for the Taking, Teaching and Learning to Give, Death*

The narrative is genealogical but it is not simply an act of memory. It *bears witness*, in the manner of an ethical or political act, for today and for tomorrow. It means first of all thinking about what takes place today. The organization of the narrative follows a genealogical detour in order to describe the current European return of mystery and orgiastic mystification; in order to describe it but more particularly to denounce, deplore, and combat it.

As the title of his essay indicates, Patočka asks why technological civilization is in decline (*úpadková*). The answer seems clear: this fall into inauthenticity indicates a return of the orgiastic or demonic. Contrary to what is normally thought, technological modernity doesn't neutralize anything; it causes a certain form of the demonic to re-emerge. Of course, it does neutralize also, by encouraging indifference and boredom, but because of that—and to the same extent in fact—it allows the return of the demonic. There is an affinity, or at least a synchrony, between a culture of boredom and an orgiastic one. The domination of technology

* The title of this chapter in the French is "Au-delà: donner à prendre, apprendre à donner—la mort."—Trans.

35

TWO

encourages demonic irresponsibility, and the sexual import of the latter does not need to be emphasized. It occurs against the background of a boredom that acts in concert with a technological leveling effect. Technological civilization only produces a heightening or recrudescence of the orgiastic, with the familiar effects of aestheticism and individualism that attend it, to the extent that it also produces boredom, for it "levels" or neutralizes the mysterious or irreplaceable uniqueness of the responsible self. The individualism of technological civilization relies precisely on a misunderstanding of the unique self. It is an individualism relating to a *role* and not a *person*. In other words it might be called the individualism of a masque or *persona*, a character [*personnage*] and not a person. Patočka reminds us of the interpretations—especially that of Burckardt—according to which modern individualism, as it has developed since the Renaissance, concerns itself with the *role that is played* rather than with this unique person whose secret remains hidden behind the social mask.

The alternatives are confused: individualism becomes socialism or collectivism, it simulates an ethics or politics of singularity; liberalism joins socialism, democracy joins totalitarianism, and all these figures share the same indifference toward everything but the objectivity of the role. Equality for all, the slogan of bourgeois revolution, becomes the objective or quantifiable equality of roles, not of persons.

This critique of the mask quite clearly harks back to a tradition, especially when it is part of a denunciation of technology in the name of an originary authenticity. Patočka is without doubt somewhat insensitive to how consistent this is, its logic seemingly uninterrupted from Plato to Heidegger. And just as the role played hides the authenticity of the irreplaceable self behind the social mask, so the civilization of boredom produced by techno-scientific objectivity hides mystery: "The most refined discoveries are boring unless they lead to an increase in the Mystery (*Tajemství*) that waits behind what is discovered, behind what is unveiled for us" (123).

Let us outline the logic of this discourse. It criticizes an inauthentic dissimulation (that is the sense common to technology,

36

role-playing, individualism, and boredom) not in the name of a revelation or truth as unveiling, but in the name of another dissimulation that, in what it holds back [*dans sa réserve même*], keeps the mystery veiled. Inauthentic dissimulation, that of the masked role, bores to the extent that it claims to unveil, show, expose, exhibit, and excite curiosity. By unveiling everything it hides that whose essence resides in its remaining hidden, namely, the authentic mystery of the person. Authentic mystery must *remain* mysterious, and we should approach it only by letting it be what it is in truth— veiled, withdrawn, dissimulated. Authentic dissimulation is inauthentically dissimulated by the violence of unveiling. The words "mystery" or "essential mystery" appear repeatedly in the final pages of Patočka's article, and its logic and intonation, at least, seem more and more Heideggerian.

Yet another concept is returned to here, and in a most decisive manner, that of force (*síla*). Everything Patočka tends to discredit—inauthenticity, technology, boredom, individualism, masks, roles—derives from a "metaphysics of force" (*Metafyzika síly*, 125). Force has become the modern figure of being. Being has allowed itself to be determined as a calculable force, and man, instead of relating to the being that is *hidden under* this figure of force, represents himself as quantifiable power. Patočka describes this definition of being as force in a schema that is analogous to that employed by Heidegger in his texts on technology:

> Man has ceased being in a relation to Being (*Bytí*) and has instead become a powerful force, one of the most powerful. [This superlative (*jednou z nejmocnějších*) indeed signifies that man has placed himself in a homogeneous relation with the forces of the world, as the strongest among those forces.] As a social entity, especially, he has become an immense transmitter sending out cosmic forces that have been stored and locked up for an eternity. It would seem that in the world of pure forces he has become a grand accumulator that on the one hand exploits these forces in order to exist and reproduce, but that on the other hand, and for the same reason, is plugged into the same circuit;

he is stored, quantified, exploited and manipulated like
any other system of forces. (124)

This description might at first seem Heideggerian, as do a number of other formulations such as "Being is sheltered in Force" or
"Force is thus found to be the most extreme withdrawal of being."
The same can be said for the idea of the dissimulation of being by
force and the dissimulation of being by the entity. One might say
that Patočka doesn't shy away from such a reading even if the
only explicit reference to Heidegger takes a strangely coded form.
Heidegger is merely *alluded to* as though, for one reason or another,
he is not to be named, whereas others like Hannah Arendt are
named, in the same context and to make a similar point. For example: "This vision of being reduced by the entity has been presented
in the work of a great contemporary thinker without credence
having been given or attention paid to it" (125). Heidegger is there,
but he is not paid any attention. He is visible but not seen. Heidegger is there like a purloined letter, he seems to say, although not
in so many words. We shall shortly witness the return of this
purloined letter.

There are however formulations that Heidegger would never
have subscribed to, for example, that which presents this metaphysics of force as a "mythology" or again as an inauthentic fiction.
"The metaphysics of force is therefore fictitious and inauthentic
[*fiktivní a nepravá*—untrue]." Heidegger would never have said
that metaphysical determinations of being or the history of the
dissimulation of being in the figures or modes of the entity developed as *myths* or *fictions*. Such terms would be more Nietzschean
than Heideggerian. And Heidegger would never have said that
metaphysics as such was of itself "untrue" or "inauthentic."

However, if one holds to the logic of (inauthentic) dissimulation
that dissimulates (authentic) dissimulation by means of the simple
gesture of exposing or exhibiting it, of seeing in order to see or
having it seen in order to see (which is the Heideggerian definition
of "curiosity"), then one has here an example of a logic of secrecy.
It is never better kept than in being exposed. Dissimulation is
never better dissimulated than by means of this particular kind of

dissimulation that consists in making a show of exposing it, unveiling it, laying it bare. The mystery of being is dissimulated by this inauthentic dissimulation that consists of exposing being as a force, showing it behind its mask, behind its fiction or its simulacrum. Is it therefore surprising to see Patočka evoke Poe's "Purloined Letter"?

> Force is thus found to be the most extreme withdrawal of being which, like the letter searched for in the story by E. A. Poe, is nowhere in a more secure place than under one's very eyes in the form of the totality of the entity, that is to say of forces that mutually organize and liberate themselves, man being no exception, deprived as he is of all things, of all mystery.
>
> This vision of being reduced by the entity has been presented in the work of a great contemporary thinker without credence having been given or attention paid to it. (125)

Heidegger *himself*, and his work, come to resemble a purloined letter. He is not only an interpreter of the play of dissimulation who can be likened to one who exposes letters; he or it is also in the place of what is called here being or the letter [*l'être ou lettre*]. This is not the first time that Heidegger and Poe are found under the same cover, folded together, for better or for worse, posthumously, in the same (hi)story of letters. Patočka does it again, warning us of this sleight of hand while also keeping Heidegger's name under wraps, performing one trick to hide another.

Since the fact of death is essential to the play of "The Purloined Letter," we are brought back to the *apprehension of death*, namely this way of *giving oneself death* that seems to imprint upon this heretical essay its dominant impulse.

What we are here calling the apprehension of death refers as much to the concern, anxious solicitude, care taken for the soul (*epimeleia tēs psykhēs*) in the *meletē thanatou*, as it does to the meaning given to death by the interpretative attitude that, in different cultures and at particular moments, for example, in orgiastic mystery, then in the Platonic *anabasis*, then in the *mysterium tremendum*, apprehends death differently, giving itself each time a different approach. The approach or apprehension of death signifies the experience of anticipation while indissociably referring to the meaning of death that is suggested in this apprehensive approach. It is always a matter of seeing coming what one can't see coming, of giving oneself that which one can probably never give oneself in a pure and simple way. Each time the self anticipates death by giving to it or conferring upon it a different value, giving itself or reappropriating what in fact it cannot simply appropriate.

The first awakening to responsibility, in its Platonic form, corresponds, for Patočka, to a conversion with respect to the experience of death. Philosophy is born out of this form of responsibility, and in the same movement philosophy is born to its own responsibility. It comes into being *as such* at the moment when the soul is not only gathering itself in the preparation for death but when it is ready to receive death, giving it to itself even, in an acceptation that delivers it from the body, and at the same time delivers it from the demonic and the orgiastic. By means of the passage to death the soul attains its own freedom.

But the *mysterium tremendum* announces, in a manner of speaking, *another death;* it announces another way of giving death or of granting oneself death. This time the word "gift" is uttered. This other way of apprehending death, and of acceding to responsibility, comes from a gift received from the other, from the one who, in absolute transcendence, sees me without my seeing, holds me in his hands while remaining inaccessible. The Christian "reversal" that converts the Platonic conversion *in turn*, involves the entrance upon the scene of a gift. An event gives the gift that transforms the Good into a Goodness that is forgetful of itself, into a love that renounces itself:

> The responsible life is itself conceived as the *gift* of something that, in the final analysis, while having the characteristics of the Good [that is, retaining, at the heart of the gift, the Platonic *agathon*], also shows traits of something inaccessible to which one must permanently submit—

traits of a mystery that has the last word. (115, my emphasis)

What is given—and this would also represent a kind of
death—is not some thing, but goodness itself, a giving goodness,
the act of giving or the donation of the gift. A goodness that must
not only forget itself but whose source remains inaccessible to the
donee. The latter receives by means of a dissymmetry of the gift
that is also a death, a death given, the gift of a death that arrives
in one way but not another. Above all it is a goodness whose
inaccessibility acts as a command to the donee. It subjects its re-
ceivers, giving itself to them as goodness itself but also as the law.
In order to understand in what way this gift of the law means not
only the emergence of a new figure of responsibility but also of
another kind of death, one has to take into account the uniqueness and irreplaceable singularity of the self as the means by
which—and it is here that it comes close to death—existence excludes every possible substitution. Now to have the experience of
responsibility on the basis of the law that is given, that is, to have
the experience of one's absolute singularity and apprehend one's
own death, amounts to the same thing. Death is very much that
which nobody else can undergo or confront in my place. My irreplaceability is therefore conferred, delivered, "given," one can say,
by death. It is the same gift, the same source, one could say the
same goodness and the same law. It is from the site of death as
the place of my irreplaceability, that is, of my singularity, that I
feel called to responsibility. In this sense only a mortal can be
responsible.

Once again, Patočka's gesture is, up to a certain point, compara-
ble to Heidegger's. In *Being and Time*, the latter passes from a
chapter where he was dealing with being-towards-death to a chapter on conscience (*Gewissen*), the call (*Ruf*), responsibility in the
face of the call, and even responsibility as originary guilt (*Schuldigsein*). And he had indeed signaled that death is the place of one's
irreplaceability. No one can die for me if "for me" means instead
of me, in my place. *"Der Tod ist, sofern er 'ist', wesensmässig je der*

meine" ("By its very essence, death is in every case mine, insofar as it 'is' at all") (§47, 240 [284]).

This formulation was preceded by a consideration of sacrifice that basically foresees—exposing itself to it but exempting itself in advance—the objection that Levinas constantly makes in relation to Heidegger, that, through the existence of the *Dasein*, he privileges "his own death."[1] Heidegger doesn't give any examples of sacrifice but one can imagine all sorts of them, in the public space of religious or political communities, in the semiprivate space of families, in the secrecy of relations between a couple (dying for God, dying for the homeland, dying to save one's children or loved one). Giving one's life *for* the other, dying *for* the other, Heidegger insists, does not mean dying in the place of the other. On the contrary, it is only to the extent that dying—insofar as it "is"—remains mine, that I can die for another or *give* my life to the other. There is no gift of self, it cannot be thought of, except in terms of this irreplaceability. Heidegger doesn't formulate it in these terms. However, it seems to me that one does not betray his thinking if one translates it in this way, for it has always, as much as has that of Levinas, paid constant attention to the fundamental and founding possibility of sacrifice. Here again, after underlining the question of irreplaceability, Heidegger defines it as the condition of possibility of sacrifice, and not of its impossibility:

> *No one can take the Other's dying away from him* (*Keiner kann dem Anderen sein Sterben abnehmen*). Of course someone can "go to his death for another" [this phrase is within quotation marks because of its almost proverbial character: to die for another ("*für einen Anderen in den Tod gehen*")]. But that always means to sacrifice oneself for the Other "*in some definite affair*" (*für den Anderen sich opfern* "in einer bestimmten Sache"). (§47, 240 [284])

Heidegger underlines *in einer bestimmten Sache*, which means "for a determinate reason," from a particular and not a total point of

---

1. Emmanuel Levinas, "La mort et le temps [Death and Time]," *L'Herne* 60 (1991), 42.

view. I can give my whole life for another, I can offer my death to the other, but in doing this I will only be replacing or saving something partial in a particular situation (there will be a nonexhaustive exchange or sacrifice, an economy of sacrifice). I know on absolute grounds and in an absolutely certain manner that I will never deliver the other from his death, from the death that affects his whole being. For these ideas concerning death are, as one well knows, motivated by Heidegger's analysis of what he calls the *Daseinsganzheit* (the totality of the *Dasein*). That is very much what is involved when to give one's life "for" the other means to give *to* death. Death's dative (dying *for* the other, giving one's life *to* the other) does not signify a substitution (*for* is not *pro* in the sense of "in place of the other"). If something radically impossible is to be conceived of—and everything derives its sense from this impossibility—it is indeed dying *for the other* in the sense of dying *in place of* the other. I can give the other everything except immortality, except this *dying for her* to the extent of dying in place of her and so freeing her from her own death. I can die for the other in a situation where my death gives him a little longer to live, I can save someone by throwing myself in the water or fire in order to temporarily snatch him from the jaws of death, I can give her my heart in the literal or figurative sense in order to assure her of a certain longevity. But I cannot die in her place, I cannot give her my life in exchange for her death. Only a mortal can die, as we said earlier. That should now be adjusted to read: and that mortal can only give to what is mortal since he can give everything except immortality, everything except salvation as immortality. In that respect we obviously remain within Heidegger's logic of sacrifice, a logic that is perhaps not that of Patočka even if he seems to follow it up to a point; nor is it that of Levinas.

But the arguments intersect in spite of their differences. They ground responsibility, as experience of singularity, in this apprehensive approach to death. The sense of responsibility is in all cases defined as a mode of "giving oneself death." Once it is established that I cannot die *for* another (in his place) although I can die *for* him (by sacrificing myself for him or dying before his eyes), my own death becomes this irreplaceability that I must assume if

I wish to have access to what is absolutely mine. My first and last responsibility, my first and last desire, is that responsibility of responsibility that relates me to what no one else can do in my place. It is thus also the very context of the *Eigentlichkeit* that, by caring, authentically relates me to my own possibility as possibility and freedom of the *Dasein*. The literality of this theme, that is essential to *Being and Time*, can be understood in its strictest sense as the irreplaceability of death:

> Such dying for (*Solches Sterben für*) can never signify that the Other has thus had his death taken away in even the slightest degree (*dem Anderen . . . abgenommen sei*). (ibid.)

This *Abnehmen* (take away, remove from) is to be compared, in the next sentence, with an *Aufnehmen*, another way of taking, taking something upon oneself, assuming, accepting. Because I cannot take death away from the other who can no more take it from me in return, it remains for everyone to take his own death *upon himself*. Everyone must assume his own death, that is to say the one thing in the world that no one else can *either give or take:* therein resides freedom and responsibility. For one can say, in French, that at least in terms of this logic, no one can either give me death or take it from me [*personne ne peut ni me donner la mort ni me prendre la mort*]. Even if one gives me death to the extent that it means killing me, that death will still have been mine and as long as it is irreducibly mine I will not have received it from anyone else. Thus dying can never be taken, borrowed, transferred, delivered, promised, or transmitted. And just as it can't be given to me, so it can't be taken away from me. Death would be this possibility of *giving and taking* [*donner-prendre*] that actually exempts itself from the same realm of possibility that it institutes, namely, from *giving and taking*. But to say that is far from contradicting the fact that it is only on the basis of death, and in its name, that *giving* and *taking* become possible.

The ideas that lead us to these last propositions, which have a literal place neither in Patočka nor in Levinas nor in Heidegger, derive from the latter's shift from *abnehmen* to *aufnehmen* in the sense of *auf sich nehmen* (to take upon oneself). The death that one cannot *abnehmen* (take from another to spare him it, no more than he can take it from me or take mine), such a death void of any possible substitution, the death that one can neither take from the other nor to the other, must be taken upon oneself (*auf sich nehmen*). Heidegger has just said that the death that "dying for" signifies in no way means death can be *abgenommen*, spared the other. More exactly: "Dying is something that every Dasein itself must take upon itself at the time" (*"Das Sterben muss jedes Dasein jeweilig selbst auf sich nehmen"*) (ibid.).

In order to put oneself to death, to give oneself death in the sense that every relation to death is an interpretative apprehension and a representative approach to death, death must be taken upon oneself. One has to *give it to oneself by taking it upon oneself*, for it can only be mine alone, irreplaceably. That is so even if, as we just said, *death can neither be taken nor given*. But the idea of being neither taken nor given relates *from* or *to* the other, and that is indeed why one can give it *to oneself* only by taking it *upon oneself*.

The question becomes concentrated in this "oneself," in the identity [*le même*] or oneself [*le soi-même*] of the mortal or dying self. "Who" or "what" gives itself death or takes it upon themselves or itself? Let us note in passing that in none of these discourses we are analyzing here does the moment of death give room for one to take into account sexual difference; as if, as it would be tempting to imagine, sexual difference does not count in the face of death. Sexual difference would be a being-*up-until*-death.

The sameness of the self, what remains irreplaceable in dying, only becomes what it is, in the sense of an identity as a relation of the self to itself, by means of this idea of mortality as irreplaceability. In the logic that Heidegger develops it is not a matter of oneself—a *Dasein* that cares—apprehending its *Jemeinigkeit* and so coming to be a being-towards-death. It is in the being-towards-death that the self of the *Jemeinigkeit* is constituted, comes into its own, that is, comes to realize its unsubstitutability. The identity of the oneself is *given* by death, by the being-towards-death that *promises* me to it. It is only to the extent that this *identity* [*ce même*] of the oneself is possible as irreducibly different singularity that death for the other or the death of the other can make sense. Such

45

an idea, in any case, never alters the oneself of the being-towards-death in the irreplaceability of the *Jemeinigkeit;* in fact it confirms it. To the extent that the mortal oneself of the *Jemeinigkeit* is originary and "nonderivable," it is indeed the place in which the call (*Ruf*) is heard and in which responsibility comes into play. In fact the *Dasein* must in the first instance answer for itself in the sameness of itself, receiving the call from nowhere else than within itself. That doesn't however prevent the call from falling upon the *Dasein:* it falls upon the *Dasein* from inside itself, it imposes itself upon it autonomously. Such is the basis for autonomy in the Kantian sense, for example: "The call comes *from* me and yet *from beyond me and over me*" ("*Der Ruf kommt* aus *mir und doch* über *mich*") (§57, 275 [320]).

One could find here the principle involved in Levinas's objection to Heidegger (we will need to come back to it later in rereading Heidegger's analysis of death as possibility of the impossibility of the *Dasein*). Levinas wants to remind us that responsibility is not at first responsibility of myself for myself, that the sameness of myself is derived from the other, as if it were second to the other, coming to itself as responsible and mortal from the position of my responsibility before the other, for the other's death and in the face of it. In the first place it is because the *other* is mortal that my responsibility is singular and "inalienable":

> I am responsible for the death of the other to the extent of including myself in that death. That can be shown in a more acceptable proposition: "I am responsible for the other inasmuch as the other is mortal." It is the other's death that is the foremost death. ("La Mort et le temps," 38)[2]

What inclusion is being talked about here? How can one be included in another's death? How can one not be? What can be meant by "including myself in that death"? Until we are able to displace the logic or topology that prevents *good sense* from thinking that or "living" it, we will have no hope of coming close to

2. The translations from Levinas are mine.—Trans. note.

Levinas's thinking, or of understanding what death teaches us [*nous ap-prend*], or gives us to think beyond the giving and taking [*donner-prendre*], in the *adieu*. What is the *adieu?* What does *adieu* mean? What does it mean to say "adieu"? How does one say and hear "*adieu*"? Not *the adieu* but *adieu?* And how can we think of death starting from *adieu* rather than the inverse?

We cannot effect such a displacement here. Let us remember however that Levinas defines the first phenomenon of death as "responselessness" in a passage in which he declares that "intentionality is not the secret of what is human" (so many paradoxical and provocative traits appear on the way to recalling the origin of responsibility): "The human *esse* is not *conatus* but disinterestedness and adieu" (25).

It seems to me that *adieu* can mean at least three things:

1. The salutation or benediction given (before all constative language "adieu" can just as well signify "hello," "I can see you," "I see that you are there," I speak to you before telling you anything else—and in certain circumstances in French it happens that one says *adieu* at the moment of meeting rather than separation);

2. The salutation or benediction given at the moment of separation, of departure, sometimes forever (this can never in fact be excluded), without any return on this earth, at the moment of death;

3. The *a-dieu*, for God or before God and before anything else or any relation to the other, in every other adieu. Every relation to the other would be, before and after anything else, an adieu.

We can only glimpse here how this idea of the adieu (of adieu) also challenges the primordial and ultimate character of the question of being or of the nondifference of the *Dasein* with respect to its own being. Levinas not only reproaches Heidegger for the fact that the *Dasein* is argued from the privileged position of its own death ("La Mort et le temps," 42) but because it gives itself death as a simple annihilation, a passage to nonbeing, which amounts to inscribing the gift of death as being-towards-death within the horizon of the question of being. On the other hand the death of the other—or for the other—that which institutes our self and our responsibility, would correspond to a more originary experience than the comprehension or precomprehension of the sense of being: "The relation to death, more ancient than any other experience, is neither vision of being or of nothingness" (25).

What is most ancient would here be the other, the possibility of dying *of* the other or *for* the other. Such a death is not given in the first instance as annihilation. It institutes responsibility as a *putting-oneself-to-death* or *offering-one's-death*, that is, *one's life*, in the ethical dimension of sacrifice.

Patočka is close to both Heidegger, whose work he knew well, and Levinas, whom he may or may not have read, but what he says differs from each of them. Even if it seems slight and secondary, the difference does not just reduce to levels of intonation or pathos. It can be quite decisive. It is not only Patočka's Christianity that separates him from those two thinkers (for argument's sake let us follow the hypothesis that in what they say in general Heidegger and Levinas are not Christian, something that is far from being clear). Along with Christianity there is a certain idea of Europe, its history and future, that also distinguishes him from them. And since Patočka's Christian politics retains something heretical about it, one might even say a decided predisposition towards a certain principle of heresy, the situation is very complicated, not to say equivocal, which makes it all the more interesting.

Let us return to those intersections of agreement and disagreement that, up to this point, have been identified in Heidegger's and Levinas's analyses of the "gift of death" that rely on responsibility. In Patočka we find all the same elements but in an overdetermined form, and thus radically transformed by his reference to a network of themes from Christianity.

The fact that Christian themes are identifiable does not mean that this text is, down to the last word and in its final signature, an essentially Christian one, even if Patočka could himself be said to be. It matters little in the end. Given that the essay involves a genealogy of European responsibility or of responsibility as Europe, of *Europe-responsibility* through the decoding of a certain history of mysteries, of their incorporation and their repression, it will always be possible to say that Patočka's text analyzes, deciphers, reconstitutes, or even deconstructs the history of this responsibility inasmuch as the latter passes through a certain history of Christianity (and who could say otherwise?). Moreover the alternative between these two hypotheses (Christian text or not, Patočka as a Christian thinker or not) is of limited pertinence. If it does involve Christianity, it is at the same time a heretical and hyperbolic form thereof. Patočka speaks and thinks in the places where Christianity has not yet thought or spoken of what it should have been and is not yet.

The Christian themes can be seen to revolve around the *gift* as gift of death, the fathomless gift of a type of death: infinite love (the Good as goodness that infinitely forgets itself), sin and salvation, repentance and sacrifice. What engenders all these meanings and links them, internally and necessarily, is a logic that at bottom (that is why it can still, up to a certain point, be called a "logic") has no need of *the event of a revelation or the revelation of an event*. It needs to think the possibility of such an event but not the event itself. This is a major point of difference, permitting such a discourse to be developed without reference to religion as institutional dogma, and proposing a genealogy of thinking concerning the possibility and essence of the religious that doesn't amount to an article of faith. If one takes into account certain differences, the same can be said for many discourses that seek in our day to be religious—discourses of a philosophical type if not philosophies themselves—without putting forth theses or *theologems* that would by their very structure teach something corresponding to the dogmas of a given religion. The difference is subtle and unstable, and it would call for careful and vigilant analyses. In different respects and with different results, the discourses of Levinas or Marion, perhaps of Ricoeur also, are in the same situation as that of Patočka. But in the final analysis this list has no clear limit and it can be said, once again taking into account the differences, that a certain Kant and a certain Hegel, Kierkegaard of course, and I might even dare to say for provocative effect, Heidegger also, belong to this tradition that consists of proposing a nondogmatic doublet of dogma, a philosophical and metaphysical doublet, in any case a *thinking* that "repeats" the possibility of religion without religion. (We will need to return to this immense and thorny question elsewhere.)

How does what we might call this logical and philosophical deduction of religious themes operate in terms of the gift of the Good as Goodness that is forgetful of itself, infinite love, gift of death, sin, repentance, sacrifice, salvation, etc.? How does such thinking elaborate, in the style of a genealogy, a reply to the question concerning what conditions render responsibility possible? The response involves [*passe*] the logical necessity of a *possibility* for the event. Everything *comes to pass* as though only the analysis of the concept of responsibility were ultimately capable of producing Christianity, or more precisely the possibility of Christianity. One might as well conclude, conversely, that this concept of responsibility is Christian through and through and is produced by the event of Christianity. For if it is as a result of examining this concept alone that the Christian event—sin, gift of infinite love linked to the experience of death—appears necessary, does that not mean that Christianity alone has made possible access to an authentic responsibility throughout history, responsibility *as history* and as history of *Europe?* There is no choice to be made here between a logical deduction, or one that is not related to the event, and the reference to a revelatory event. One implies the other. And it is not simply as a believer or as a Christian affirming dogma, the revelation, and the event, that Patočka makes the declaration already referred to, as would a genealogist historian stating what point history has arrived at:

> Because of its foundation within the abyssal profundity of the soul, Christianity represents to this day the most powerful means—never yet superseded but not yet thought right through either—by which man is able to struggle against his own decline. (117)

On what condition is responsibility possible? On the condition that the Good no longer be a transcendental objective, a relation between objective things, but the relation to the other, a response to the other; an experience of personal goodness and a movement of intention. That supposes, as we have seen, a double rupture: both with orgiastic mystery *and* with Platonism. On what condition does goodness exist beyond all calculation? On the condition that goodness forget itself, that the movement be a movement of the gift that renounces itself, hence a movement of infinite love. Only infinite love can renounce itself and, in order to *become finite*, become incarnated in order to love the other, to love the other as a finite other. This gift of infinite love comes from someone and is addressed to someone; responsibility demands irreplaceable singularity. Yet only death or rather the apprehension of death can give this irreplaceability, and it is only on the basis of it that one can speak of a responsible subject, of the soul as conscience of self, of myself, etc. We have thus deduced the possibility of a mortal's accession to responsibility through the experience of his irreplaceability, that which an approaching death or the approach of death gives him. But the mortal thus deduced is someone whose very responsibility requires that he concern himself not only with an objective Good but with a gift of infinite love, a goodness that is forgetful of itself. There is thus a structural disproportion or dissymmetry between the finite and responsible mortal on the one hand and the goodness of the infinite gift on the other hand. One can conceive of this disproportion without assigning to it a revealed cause or without tracing it back to the event of original sin, but it inevitably transforms the experience of responsibility into one of guilt: I have never been and never will be up to the level of this infinite goodness nor up to the immensity of the gift, the frameless immensity that must in general define (*in*-define) a gift as such. This guilt is originary, like original sin. Before any fault is determined, I am guilty inasmuch as I am responsible. What gives me my singularity, namely, death and finitude, is what makes me unequal to the infinite goodness of the gift that is also the first appeal to responsibility. Guilt is inherent in responsibility because responsibility is always unequal to itself: one is never responsible enough. One is never responsible enough because one is finite but also because responsibility requires two contradictory movements. It requires one to respond as oneself and as irreplaceable singularity, to answer for what one does, says, gives; but it also requires that, being good and through goodness, one forget or efface the origin of what one gives. Patočka doesn't say that in so many words, and I am stretching things a little further than he or the letter of his text would allow. But it is he who deduces guilt and sin—and so repentance, sacrifice, and the seeking of salvation—in the situation of the responsible individual:

> The responsible man as such is a *self*, an individual that doesn't coincide with any role that he might happen to assume [an interior and invisible self, a secret self at bottom]—something Plato expresses through the myth of the choice of destiny [a *pre*-Christian myth then, one that prepares for Christianity]; he is a responsible self because, in confronting death and in dealing with nothingness [a more "Heideggerian" than "Levinasian" theme], he takes upon himself what only each one of us can realize in ourselves, that which makes each of us irreplaceable. Now, however, individuality has been related to infinite love and man is an individual because he is guilty, *always* guilty with respect to that love. [Patočka emphasizes "always": like Heidegger he defines there an originary guilt that doesn't wait for one to commit any particular fault, crime, or sin, an a priori guilt that is included in the conception of responsibility, in the originary *Schuldigsein*, which one can translate as "responsibility" as well as "guilt." But Heidegger has no need to make reference, no explicit reference at least, to this disproportion with respect to an infinite love in order to analyze the originary *Schuldigsein*.] Each is determined as individual by the uniqueness of what situates him in the generality of sin. (116)

THREE

Whom to Give to (Knowing Not to Know)

Mysterium tremendum. A frightful mystery, a secret to make you tremble.

Tremble. What does one do when one trembles? What is it that makes you tremble?

A secret always *makes* you tremble. Not simply quiver or shiver, which also happens sometimes, but tremble. A quiver can of course manifest fear, anguish, apprehension of death; as when one quivers in advance, in anticipation of what is to come. But it can be slight, on the surface of the skin, like a quiver that announces the arrival of pleasure or an orgasm. It is a moment in passing, the suspended time of seduction. A quiver is not always very serious, it is sometimes discreet, barely discernible, somewhat epiphenomenal. It prepares for, rather than follows the event. One could say that water quivers before it boils; that is the idea I was referring to as seduction: a superficial pre-boil, a preliminary and visible agitation.

On the other hand, trembling, at least as a signal or symptom, is something that has already taken place, as in the case of an earthquake [*tremblement de terre*] or when one trembles all over. It is no longer preliminary even if, unsettling everything so as to imprint upon the body an irrepressible shaking, the event that makes one tremble portends and threatens still. It suggests that violence is going to break out again, that some traumatism will insist on being repeated. As different as dread, fear, anxiety, terror, panic, or anguish remain from one another, they have already begun in the trembling, and what has provoked them continues, or threatens to continue, to make us tremble. Most often we neither know what is coming upon us nor see its origin; it therefore remains a secret. We are afraid of the fear, we anguish over the anguish, and we tremble. We tremble in that strange repetition that ties an irrefutable past (a shock has been felt, a traumatism has already affected us) to a future that cannot be anticipated; anticipated but unpredictable; *apprehended*, but, and this is why there is a future, apprehended precisely *as* unforeseeable, unpredictable; approached *as* unapproachable. Even if one thinks one knows what is going to happen, the new instant of that happening remains untouched, still unaccessible, in fact unlivable. In the repetition of what still remains unpredictable, we tremble first of all because we don't know from which direction the shock came, whence it was given (whether a good surprise or a bad shock, sometimes a surprise received as a shock); and we tremble from not knowing, in the form of a double secret, whether it is going to continue, start again, insist, be repeated: whether it will, how it will, where, when; and why *this* shock. Hence I tremble because I am still afraid of what already makes me afraid, of what I can neither see nor foresee. I tremble at what exceeds my seeing and my knowing [*mon voir et mon savoir*] although it concerns the innermost parts of me, right down to my soul, down to the bone, as we say. Inasmuch as it tends to undo both seeing and knowing, trembling is indeed an experience of secrecy or of mystery, but another secret, another enigma, or another mystery comes on top of the unlivable experience, adding yet another seal or concealment to the *tremor* (the Latin word for "trembling," from *tremo*, which in Greek as in Latin means *I tremble, I am afflicted by trembling*; in Greek there is also *tromeō*: I tremble, I shiver, I am afraid; and *tromos*, which means trembling, fear, fright. In Latin, *tremendus, tremendum*, as in *mysterium tremendum*, is a gerundive derived from *tremo:* what makes one tremble, something frightening, distressing, terrifying).

Where does this supplementary seal come from? One doesn't know *why one trembles.* This limit to knowledge no longer only relates to the cause or unknown event, the unseen or unknown that makes us tremble. Neither do we know why it produces this particular symptom, a certain irrepressible agitation of the body, the uncontrollable instability of its members or of the substance of the skin or muscles. Why does the irrepressible take this form? Why does terror make us tremble, since one can also tremble with cold, and such analogous physiological manifestations translate experiences and sentiments that appear, at least, not to have anything in common? This symptomatology is as enigmatic as tears. Even if one knows why one weeps, in what situation, and what it signifies (I weep because I have lost one of my nearest and dearest, the child cries because he has been beaten or because she is not loved: she causes herself grief, complains, he makes himself complain or allows himself to be felt sorry for—by means of the other), but that still doesn't explain why the lachrymal glands come to secrete these drops of water which are brought to the eyes rather than elsewhere, the mouth or the ears. We would need to make new inroads into thinking concerning the body, without dissociating the registers of discourse (thought, philosophy, the bio-genetico-psychoanalytic sciences, phylo- and ontogenesis), in order to one day come closer to what makes us tremble or what makes us cry, to that *cause* which is not the final cause that can be called God or death (God is the cause of the *mysterium tremendum,* and the death that is given is always what makes us tremble, or what makes us weep as well) but to a closer cause; not the immediate cause, that is, the accident or circumstance, but the cause closest to our body, that which means that one trembles or weeps rather than doing something else. What is it a metaphor or figure for? What does *the body mean to say* by trembling or crying, presuming one can speak here of the body, or of saying, of meaning, and of rhetoric?

What is it that makes us tremble in the *mysterium tremendum?* It is the gift of infinite love, the dissymmetry that exists between the divine regard that sees me, and myself, who doesn't see what is looking at me; it is the gift and endurance of death that exists in the irreplaceable, the disproportion between the infinite gift and my finitude, responsibility as culpability, sin, salvation, repentance, and sacrifice. As in the title of Kierkegaard's essay *Fear and Trembling*,[1] the *mysterium tremendum* includes at least an implicit and indirect reference to Saint Paul. In the Epistle to the Philippians 2: 12, the disciples are asked to work towards their salvation in fear and trembling. They will have to work for their salvation knowing all along that it is God who decides: the Other has no reason to give to us and nothing to settle in our favor, no reason to share his reasons with us. We fear and tremble because we are already in the hands of God, although free to work, but in the hands and under the gaze of God, whom we don't see and whose will we cannot know, no more than the decisions he will hand down, nor his reasons for wanting this or that, our life or death, our salvation or perdition. We fear and tremble before the inaccessible secret of a God who decides for us although we remain responsible, that is, free to decide, to work, to assume our life and our death.

So Paul says—and this is one of the "adieux" I spoke of earlier:

> Wherefore my beloved, as ye have always obeyed, not as in my presence only, but now much more in my absence (*non ut in praesentia mei tantum, sed multo magis nunc in absentia mea / mē hōs en tē parousia mou monon alla nun pollō mallon en tē apousia mou*), work out your own salvation with fear and trembling (*cum metu et tremore / meta phobou kai tromou*).[2]

This is a first explanation of the fear and of the trembling, and of "fear and trembling." The disciples are asked to work towards their salvation not in the presence (*parousia*) but in the absence

---

1. Søren Kierkegaard, *Fear and Trembling, and Repetition*, vol. 6, *Kierkegaard's Writings*, ed. and trans. Howard V. Hong and Edna H. Hong (Princeton: Princeton University Press, 1983). Page references are to this edition.

2. Philippians 2: 12. All biblical quotations are from the King James version.—Trans. note.

(*apousia*) of the master: without either seeing or knowing, without hearing the law or the reasons for the law. Without knowing from whence the thing comes and what awaits us, we are given over to absolute solitude. No one can speak with us and no one can speak for us; we must take it upon ourselves, each of us must take it upon himself (*auf sich nehmen* as Heidegger says concerning death, our death, concerning what is always "my death," and which no one can take on in place of me). But there is something even more serious at the origin of this trembling. If Paul says "adieu" and absents himself as he asks them to obey, in fact ordering them to obey (for one doesn't ask for obedience, one orders it), it is because God is himself absent, hidden and silent, separate, secret, at the moment he has to be obeyed. God doesn't give his reasons, he acts as he intends, he doesn't have to give his reasons or share anything with us: neither his motivations, if he has any, nor his delib-erations, nor his decisions. Otherwise he wouldn't be God, we wouldn't be dealing with the Other as God or with God as *wholly other* [*tout autre*]. If the other were to share his reasons with us by explaining them to us, if he were to speak to us all the time without any secrets, he wouldn't be the other, we would share a type of homogeneity. Discourse also partakes of that sameness; we don't speak with God or to God, we don't speak with God or to God as with others or to our fellows. Paul continues in fact:

> For it is God which worketh in you both to will and to
> do of his good pleasure. (Philippians 2: 13)[3]

One can understand why Kierkegaard chose, for his title, the words of a great Jewish convert, Paul, in order to meditate on the

3. I am following the Grosjean and Léturmy translation (Bibliothèque de la Pléiade) here, and will often find it necessary to add Greek or Latin glosses. What they translate by *son bon plaisir* ("his good pleasure") doesn't refer to God's pleasure but to his sovereign will that is not required to consult, just as the king acts as he intends without revealing his secret reasons, without having to account for his actions or explain them. The text doesn't name God's pleasure but his will: *pro bona voluntate* or *hyper tēs eudokias: Eudokia* means "good will," not just in the sense of desiring the good, but as the will that judges well, for its pleasure, as in their translation; for that is his will and it suffices. *Eudokeō:* "I judge well," "I approve," sometimes "I am pleased" or "I take pleasure in," "I consent."

still Jewish experience of a secret, hidden, separate, absent, or mysterious God, the one who decides, without revealing his reasons, to demand of Abraham that most cruel, impossible, and untenable gesture: to offer his son Isaac as a sacrifice. All that goes on in secret. God keeps silent about his reasons. Abraham does also, and the book is not signed by Kierkegaard, but by Johannes de Silentio ("a poetic person who only exists among poets," Kierkegaard writes in the margin of his text (Pap. IV B 79, *Fear and Trembling*, 243).

This pseudonym keeps silent, it expresses the silence that is kept. Like all pseudonyms, it seems destined to keep secret the real name *as* patronym, that is, the name of the father of the work, in fact the name of the father of the father of the work. This pseudonym, one among many that Kierkegaard employed, reminds us that a meditation linking the question of secrecy to that of responsibility immediately raises the question of the name and of the signature. One often thinks that responsibility consists of acting and signing *in one's name*. A responsible reflection on responsibility is interested in advance in whatever happens to the name in the event of pseudonymity, metonymy, homonymy, in the matter of what constitutes *a real name*. Sometimes one says or wishes it more effectively, more authentically, in the secret name by which *one calls oneself*, that *one gives oneself or affects to give oneself*, the name that is more *naming* and *named* in the pseudonym than in the official legality of the public patronym.

The trembling of *Fear and Trembling*, is, or so it seems, the very experience of sacrifice. Not, first of all, in the Hebraic sense of the term, *korban*, which refers more to an approach or a "coming close to," and which has been wrongly translated as "sacrifice," but in the sense that sacrifice supposes the putting to death of the unique in terms of its being unique, irreplaceable, and most precious. It also therefore refers to the impossibility of substitution, the unsubstitutable; and then also to the substitution of an animal for man; and finally, especially this, by means of this impossible substitution itself, it refers to what links the sacred to sacrifice and sacrifice to secrecy.

Kierkegaard-de Silentio recalls Abraham's strange reply to Isaac when the latter asks him where the sacrificial lamb is to be found. It can't be said that Abraham doesn't respond to him. He says God will provide. God will provide a lamb for the holocaust (["burnt offering"] Genesis 22: 8). Abraham thus keeps his secret at the same time as he replies to Isaac. He doesn't keep silent and he doesn't lie. He doesn't speak nontruth. In *Fear and Trembling* (*Problema III*) Kierkegaard reflects on this double secret: that between God and Abraham but also that between the latter and his family. Abraham doesn't speak of what God has ordered him alone to do, he doesn't speak of it to Sarah, or to Eliezer, or to Isaac. He must keep the secret (that is his duty), but it is also a secret that he *must* keep as a double necessity because in the end he *can only* keep it: he doesn't know it, he is unaware of its ultimate rhyme and reason. He is sworn to secrecy because he is in secret.

Because, in this way, he doesn't speak, Abraham transgresses the ethical order. According to Kierkegaard, the highest expression of the ethical is in terms of what binds us to our own and to our fellows (that can be the family but also the actual community of friends or the nation). By keeping the secret, Abraham betrays ethics. His silence, or at least the fact that he doesn't divulge the secret of the sacrifice he has been asked to make, is certainly not designed to save Isaac.

Of course, in some respects Abraham does speak. He says a lot. But even if he says everything, he need only keep silent on a single thing for one to conclude that he hasn't spoken. Such a silence takes over his whole discourse. So he speaks and doesn't speak. He responds without responding. He responds and doesn't respond. He responds indirectly. He speaks in order not to say anything about the essential thing that he must keep secret. Speaking in order not to say anything is always the best technique for keeping a secret. Still, Abraham doesn't just speak in order not to say anything when he replies to Isaac. He says something that is not nothing and that is not false. He says something that is not a non-truth, something moreover that, although *he doesn't know it yet,* will turn out to be true.

To the extent that, in not saying the essential thing, namely, the secret between God and him, Abraham doesn't speak, he assumes the responsibility that consists in always being alone, entrenched in one's own singularity at the moment of decision. Just as no one can die in my place, no one can make a decision, what we call "a decision," in my place. But as soon as one speaks, as soon as one enters the medium of language, one loses that very singularity. One therefore loses the possibility of deciding or the right to decide. Thus every decision would, fundamentally, remain at the same time solitary, secret, and silent. Speaking relieves us, Kierkegaard notes, for it "translates" into the general (113).[4]

The first effect or first destination of language therefore involves depriving me of, or delivering me from, my singularity. By suspending my absolute singularity in speaking, I renounce at the same time my liberty and my responsibility. Once I speak I am never and no longer myself, alone and unique. It is a very strange contract—both paradoxical and terrifying—that binds infinite responsibility to silence and secrecy. It goes against what one usually thinks, even in the most philosophical mode. For common sense, just as for philosophical reasoning, the most widely shared belief is that responsibility is tied to the public and to the nonsecret, to the possibility and even the necessity of accounting for one's words and actions in front of others, of justifying and owning up to them. Here on the contrary it appears, just as necessarily, that the absolute responsibility of my actions, to the extent that such a responsibility remains mine, singularly so, something no one else can perform in my place, instead implies secrecy. But what is also implied is that, by not speaking to others, I don't account for my actions, that I answer for nothing [*que je ne réponde de rien*] and to no one, that I make no response to others or before others. It is both a scandal and a paradox. According to Kierkegaard, *ethical* exigency is regulated by generality; and it therefore defines a responsibility that consists of *speaking*, that is, of involving oneself sufficiently in the generality to justify oneself, to give an acccount

4. The English translation gives "the universal" for *det Almene*, whereas "the general" is closer to the Danish and is the term Derrida uses. Note also Kierkegaard's distinction between *individuel* ("individual") and *enkelt* ("singular") that anticipates Derrida's here. For this and other clarifications of the English translation I am grateful to Elsebet Jegstrup and Mark Taylor.—Trans. note.

of one's decision and to answer for one's actions. On the other hand, what does Abraham teach us, in his approach to sacrifice? That far from ensuring responsibility, the generality of ethics incites to irresponsibility. It impels me to speak, to reply, to account for something, and thus to dissolve my singularity in the medium of the concept.

Such is the aporia of responsibility: one always risks not managing to accede to the concept of responsibility in the process of *forming* it. For responsibility (we would no longer dare speak of "the universal concept of responsibility") demands on the one hand an accounting, a general answering-for-oneself with respect to the general and before the generality, hence the idea of substitution, and, on the other hand, uniqueness, absolute singularity, hence nonsubstitution, nonrepetition, silence, and secrecy. What I am saying here about responsibility can also be said about decision. The ethical involves me in substitution, as does speaking. Whence the insolence of the paradox: for Abraham, Kierkegaard declares, *the ethical is a temptation.* He must therefore resist it. He keeps quiet in order to avoid the moral temptation which, under the pretext of calling him to responsibility, to self-justification, would make him lose his ultimate responsibility along with his singularity, make him lose his unjustifiable, secret, and absolute responsibility before God. This is ethics as "irresponsibilization," as an insoluble and paradoxical contradiction between responsibility *in general* and *absolute* responsibility. Absolute responsibility is not a responsibility, at least it is not general responsibility or responsibility in general. It needs to be exceptional or extraordinary, and it needs to be that absolutely and par excellence: it is as if absolute responsibility could not be derived from a *concept* of responsibility and therefore, in order for it to be what it must be it must remain inconceivable, indeed unthinkable: it must therefore be irresponsible in order to be absolutely responsible. "Abraham *cannot* speak, because he cannot say that which would explain everything . . . that it is an ordeal such that, please note, the ethical is the temptation" (115).

The ethical can therefore end up making us irresponsible. It is a temptation, a tendency, or a facility that would sometimes have to be refused in the name of a responsibility that doesn't keep account or give an account, neither to man, to humans, to society, to one's fellows, or to one's own. Such a responsibility keeps its secret, it cannot and need not present itself. Tyrannically, jealously, it refuses to present itself before the violence that consists of asking for accounts and justifications, summonses to appear before the law of men. It declines the autobiography that is always auto-justification, *égodicée*. Abraham *presents himself*, of course, but before God, the unique, jealous, secret God, the one to whom he says "Here I am." But in order to do that, he must renounce his family loyalties, which amounts to violating his oath, and refuse to present himself before men. He no longer speaks to them. That at least is what the sacrifice of Isaac suggests (it would be different for a tragic hero such as Agamemnon).

In the end secrecy is as intolerable for ethics as it is for philosophy or for dialectics in general, from Plato to Hegel:

> The ethical as such is the universal; as the universal it is in turn the disclosed. The single individual, qualified as immediate, sensate, and psychical, is the hidden. Thus his ethical task is to work himself out of his hiddenness and to become disclosed in the universal. Every time he desires to remain in the hidden, he trespasses and is immersed in spiritual trial from which he can emerge only by disclosing himself.
>
> Once again we stand at the same point. If there is no hiddenness rooted in the fact that the single individual as the single individual is higher than the universal, then Abraham's conduct cannot be defended, for he disregarded the intermediary ethical categories. But if there is such a hiddenness, then we face the paradox, which does not allow itself to be mediated, since it is based precisely on this: the single individual as the single individual is higher than the universal. . . . The Hegelian philosophy assumes no justified hiddenness, no justified incommensurability. It is, then, consistent for it to demand disclosure, but it is a little bemuddled when it wants to regard Abra-

ham as the father of faith and to speak about faith. (82, translation modified—DW)

In the exemplary form of its absolute coherence, Hegel's philosophy represents the irrefutable demand for manifestation, phenomenalization, and unveiling; thus, it is thought, it represents the request for truth that inspires philosophy and ethics in their most powerful forms. There are no final secrets for philosophy, ethics, or politics. The manifest is given priority over the hidden or the secret, universal generality is superior to the individual; no irreducible secret that can be legally justified (*fondé en droit* says the French translation of Kierkegaard)—and thus the instance of the law has to be added to those of philosophy and ethics; nothing hidden, no absolutely legitimate secret. But the paradox of faith is that interiority remains "incommensurable with exteriority" (69). No manifestation can consist in rendering the interior exterior or show what is hidden. The knight of faith can neither communicate to nor be understood by anyone, she can't help the other at all (71). The absolute duty that obligates her with respect to God cannot have the form of generality that is called duty. If I obey in my duty towards God (which is my absolute duty) *only in terms of duty*, I am not fulfilling my relation to God. In order to fulfill my duty towards God, I must not act *out of duty*, by means of that form of generality that can always be mediated and communicated and that is called duty. The absolute duty that binds me to God himself, in faith, must function beyond and against any duty I have. "The duty becomes duty by being traced back to God, but in the duty itself I do not enter into relation to God" (68). Kant explains that to act morally is to act "out of duty" and not only "by conforming to duty." Kierkegaard sees acting "out of duty," in the universalizable sense of the law, as a dereliction of one's absolute duty. It is in this sense that absolute duty (towards God and in the singularity of faith) implies a sort of gift or sacrifice that functions beyond both debt and duty, beyond duty as a form of debt. This is the dimension that provides for a "gift of death" which, beyond human responsibility, beyond the universal concept of duty, is a response to absolute duty.

In the order of human generality, a duty of hate is implied. Kierkegaard quotes Luke 14:26: " 'If any one comes to me and does not hate his own father and mother and his wife and children and brothers and sisters, yes, and even his own life, he cannot be my disciple'." Recognizing that "this is a hard saying" (72), Kierkegaard nevertheless upholds the necessity for it. He refines its rigor without seeking to make it less shocking or paradoxical. But Abraham's hatred for the ethical and thus for his own (family, friends, neighbors, nation, but at the outside humanity as a whole, his own kind or species) must remain an absolute source of pain. If I put to death or grant death to what I hate it is not a sacrifice. I must sacrifice what I love. I must come to hate what I love, in the same moment, at the instant of granting death. I must hate and betray my own, that is to say offer them the gift of death by means of the sacrifice, not insofar as I hate them, that would be too easy, but insofar as I love them. I must hate them insofar as I love them. Hate wouldn't be hate if it only hated the hateful, that would be too easy. It must hate and betray what is most lovable. Hate cannot be hate, it can only be the sacrifice of love to love. It is not a matter of hating, betraying by one's breach of trust, or offering the gift of death to what one doesn't love.

But is this heretical and paradoxical knight of faith Jewish, Christian, or Judeo-Christian-Islamic? The sacrifice of Isaac belongs to what one might just dare to call the common treasure, the terrifying secret of the *mysterium tremendum* that is a property of all three so-called religions of the Book, the religions of the races of Abraham. This rigor, and the exaggerated demands it entails, compel the knight of faith to say and do things that will appear (and must even be) atrocious. They will necessarily revolt those who profess allegiance to morality in general, to Judeo-Christian-Islamic morality, or to the religion of love in general. But as Patočka will say, perhaps Christianity has not yet thought through its own essence, any more than it has thought through the irrefutable events through which Judaism, Christianity, and Islam have come to pass. One cannot ignore or erase the sacrifice of Isaac recounted in Genesis, nor that recounted in the Gospel of Luke. It has to be taken into account, which is what Kierkegaard proposes.

Abraham comes to hate those closest to him by keeping silent, he comes to hate his only beloved son by consenting to put him to death [*lui donner la mort*]. He hates them not out of hatred, of course, but out of love. He doesn't hate them any less for all that, on the contrary. Abraham must love his son absolutely to come to the point where he will grant him death, to commit what ethics would call hatred and murder.

How does one hate one's own? Kierkegaard rejects the common distinction between love and hate; he finds it egotistical and without interest. He reinterprets it as a paradox. God wouldn't have asked Abraham to put Isaac to death, that is, to make a gift of death as a sacrificial offering to himself, to God, unless Abraham had an absolute, unique, and incommensurable love for his son:

> for it is indeed this love for Isaac that makes his act a sacrifice by its paradoxical contrast to his love for God. But the distress and the anxiety in the paradox is that he, humanly speaking, is thoroughly incapable of making himself understandable. Only *in the instant* when his act is in absolute contradiction to his feelings, only then does he sacrifice Isaac, but the reality of his act is that by which he belongs to the universal, and there he is and remains a murderer. (74, translation modified—DW)

I have emphasized the word *instant:* "the instant of decision is madness," Kierkegaard says elsewhere. The paradox cannot be grasped in time and through mediation, that is to say in language and through reason. Like the gift and "the gift of death," it remains irreducible to presence or to presentation, it demands a temporality of the instant without ever constituting a present. If it can be said, it belongs to an atemporal temporality, to a duration that cannot be grasped: something one can neither stabilize, establish, *grasp* [*prendre*], apprehend, or *comprehend*. Understanding, common sense, and reason cannot seize [*begreifen*], conceive, understand, or mediate it; neither can they negate or deny it, implicate it in the work of negation, make it work: in the act of *giving death*, sacrifice suspends both the work of negation and work itself, perhaps even the work of mourning. The tragic hero enters into mourning. Abraham, on the other hand, is neither a man of mourning nor a tragic hero.

In order to assume his absolute responsibility with respect to absolute duty, to put his faith in God to work, or to the test, he must also in reality remain a hateful murderer, for he consents to put to death. In both general and abstract terms, the absoluteness of duty, of responsibility, and of obligation certainly demands that one transgress ethical duty, although in betraying it one belongs to it and at the same time recognizes it. The contradiction and the paradox must be endured *in the instant itself.* The two duties must contradict one another, one must subordinate (incorporate, repress) the other. Abraham must assume absolute responsibility for sacrificing his son by sacrificing ethics, but in order for there to be a sacrifice, the ethical must retain all its value; the love for his son must remain intact, and the order of human duty must continue to insist on its rights.

The account of Isaac's sacrifice can be read as a narrative development of the paradox constituting the concept of duty and absolute responsibility. This concept puts us into relation (but without relating to it, in a double secret) with the absolute other, with the absolute singularity of the other, whose name here is God. Whether one believes the biblical story or not, whether one gives it credence, doubts it, or transposes it, it could still be said that there is a moral to this story, even if we take it to be a fable (but taking it to be a fable still amounts to losing it to philosophical or poetic generality; it means that it loses the quality of a historic event). The moral of the fable would be morality itself, at the point where morality brings into play the gift of the death that is so given. The absolutes of duty and of responsibility presume that one denounce, refute, and transcend, at the same time, all duty, all responsibility, and every human law. It calls for a betrayal of everything that manifests itself within the order of universal generality, and everything that manifests itself in general, the very order and essence of manifestation; namely, the essence itself, the essence in general to the extent that it is inseparable from presence and from manifestation. Absolute duty demands that one behave in an irresponsible manner (by means of treachery or betrayal), while still recognizing, confirming, and reaffirming the very thing one sacrifices, namely, the order of human ethics and responsibility. In a word, ethics must be sacrificed in the name of duty. It is a duty not to respect, out of duty, ethical duty. One must behave not only in an ethical or responsible manner, but in a nonethical, nonresponsible manner, and one must do that *in the name of* duty, of an infinite duty, *in the name of* absolute duty. And this name which must always be singular is here none other than the name of God as completely other, the nameless name of God, the unpronounceable name of God as other to which I am bound by an absolute, unconditional obligation, by an incomparable, nonnegotiable duty. The other as absolute other, namely, God, must remain transcendent, hidden, secret, jealous of the love, requests, and commands that he gives and that he asks to be kept secret. Secrecy is essential to the exercise of this absolute responsibility as sacrificial responsibility.

In terms of the moral of morality, let us here insist upon what is too often forgotten by the moralizing moralists and good consciences who preach to us with assurance every morning and every week, in newspapers and magazines, on the radio and on television, about the sense of ethical or political responsibility. Philosophers who don't write ethics are failing in their duty, one often hears, and the first duty of the philosopher is to think about ethics, to add a chapter on ethics to each of his or her books and, in order to do that, to come back to Kant as often as possible. What the knights of good conscience don't realize, is that "the sacrifice of Isaac" illustrates—if that is the word in the case of such a nocturnal mystery—the most common and everyday experience of responsibility. The story is no doubt monstrous, outrageous, barely conceivable: a father is ready to put to death his beloved son, his irreplaceable loved one, and that because the Other, the great Other asks him or orders him without giving the slightest explanation. An infanticide father who hides what he is going to do from his son and from his family without knowing why, what could be more abominable, what mystery could be more frightful (*tremendum*) vis-à-vis love, humanity, the family, or morality?

But isn't this also the most common thing? what the most cursory examination of the concept of responsibility cannot fail to affirm? Duty or responsibility binds me to the other, to the other as other, and ties me in my absolute singularity to the other as other. God is the name of the absolute other as other and as unique (the God of Abraham defined as the one and unique). As soon as I enter into a relation with the absolute other, my absolute singularity enters into relation with his on the level of obligation and duty. I am responsible to the other as other, I answer to him and I answer for what I do before him. But of course, what binds me thus in my singularity to the absolute singularity of the other, immediately propels me into the space or risk of absolute sacrifice. There are also others, an infinite number of them, the innumerable generality of others to whom I should be bound by the same responsibility, a general and universal responsibility (what Kierkegaard calls the ethical order). I cannot respond to the call, the request, the obligation, or even the love of another without sacrificing the other other, the other others. *Every other (one) is every (bit) other* [*tout autre est tout autre*], every one else is completely or wholly other. The simple concepts of alterity and of singularity constitute the concept of duty as much as that of responsibility. As a result, the concepts of responsibility, of decision, or of duty, are condemned a priori to paradox, scandal, and aporia. Paradox, scandal, and aporia are themselves nothing other than sacrifice, the revelation of conceptual thinking at its limit, at its death and finitude. As soon as I enter into a relation with the other, with the gaze, look, request, love, command, or call of the other, I know that I can respond only by sacrificing ethics, that is, by sacrificing whatever obliges me to also respond, in the same way, in the same instant, to all the others. I offer a gift of death, I betray, I don't need to raise my knife over my son on Mount Moriah for that. Day and night, at every instant, on all the Mount Moriahs of this world, I am doing that, raising my knife over what I love and must love, over those to whom I owe absolute fidelity, incommensurably. Abraham is faithful to God only in his absolute treachery, in the betrayal of his own and of the uniqueness of each one of them, exemplified here in his only beloved son. He would not be able to opt for fidelity to his own, or to his son, unless he were to betray the absolute other: God, if you wish.

Let us not look for examples, there would be too many of them, at every step we took. By preferring my work, simply by giving it my time and attention, by preferring my activity as a citizen or as a professorial and professional philosopher, writing and speaking here in a public language, French in my case, I am perhaps fulfilling my duty. But I am sacrificing and betraying at every moment all my other obligations: my obligations to the other others whom I know or don't know, the billions of my fellows (without mentioning the animals that are even more other others than my fellows), my fellows who are dying of starvation or sickness. I betray my fidelity or my obligations to other citizens, to those who don't speak my language and to whom I neither speak nor respond, to each of those who listen or read, and to whom I neither respond nor address myself in the proper manner, that is, in a singular manner (this for the so-called public space to which I sacrifice my so-called private space), thus also to those I love in private, my own, my family, my son, each of whom is the only son I sacrifice to the other, every one being sacrificed to every one else in this land of Moriah that is our habitat every second of every day.

This is not just a figure of style or an effect of rhetoric. According to 2 Chronicles, 3 and 8, the place where this occurs, where the sacrifice of Abraham or of Isaac (and it is the sacrifice of both of them, it is the gift of death one makes to the other in putting *oneself* to death, mortifying oneself in order to make a gift of this death as a sacrificial offering to God) takes place, this place where death is given or offered, is the place where Solomon decided to build the House of the Lord in Jerusalem, also the place where God appeared to Solomon's father, David. However, it is also the place where the grand Mosque of Jerusalem stood, the place called the Dome of the Rock near the grand Aksa mosque where the sacrifice of Ibrahim is supposed to have taken place and from where Muhammad mounted his horse for paradise after his death. It is just above the destroyed temple of Jerusalem and the

Wailing Wall, not far from the Way of the Cross. It is therefore a holy place but also a place that is in dispute, radically and rabidly, fought over by all the monotheisms, by all the religions of the unique and transcendent God, of the absolute other. These three monotheisms fight over it, it is useless to deny this in terms of some wide-eyed ecumenism; they make war with fire and blood, have always done so and all the more fiercely today, each claiming its particular perspective on this place and claiming an original historical and political interpretation of Messianism and of the sacrifice of Isaac. The reading, interpretation, and tradition of the sacrifice of Isaac are themselves sites of bloody, holocaustic sacrifice. Isaac's sacrifice continues every day. Countless machines of death wage a war that has no front. There is no front between responsibility and irresponsibility but only between different appropriations of the same sacrifice, different orders of responsibility, different other orders: the religious and the ethical, the religious and the ethico-political, the theological and the political, the theologico-political, the theocratic and the ethico-political, and so on; the secret and the public, the profane and the sacred, the specific and the generic, the human and the nonhuman. Sacrificial war rages not only among the religions of the Book and the races of Abraham that expressly refer to the sacrifice of Isaac, Abraham, or Ibrahim, but between them and the rest of the starving world, within the immense majority of humankind and even those living (not to mention the others, dead or nonliving, dead or not yet born) who don't belong to the people of Abraham or Ibrahim, all those others to whom the names of Abraham and Ibrahim have never meant anything because such names don't conform or correspond to anything.

I can respond only to the one (or to the One), that is, to the other, by sacrificing that one to the other. I am responsible to any one (that is to say to any other) only by failing in my responsibilities to all the others, to the ethical or political generality. And I can never justify this sacrifice, I must always hold my peace about it. Whether I want to or not, I can never justify the fact that I prefer or sacrifice any one (any other) to the other. I will always be secretive, held to secrecy in respect of this, for I have nothing

WHOM TO GIVE TO

to say about it. What binds me to singularities, to this one or that one, male or female, rather than that one or this one, remains finally unjustifiable (this is Abraham's hyper-ethical sacrifice), as unjustifiable as the infinite sacrifice I make at each moment. These singularities represent others, a wholly other form of alterity: one other or some other persons, but also places, animals, languages. How would you ever justify the fact that you sacrifice all the cats in the world to the cat that you feed at home every morning for years, whereas other cats die of hunger at every instant? Not to mention other people? How would you justify your presence here speaking one particular language, rather than there speaking to others in another language? And yet we also do our duty by behaving thus. There is no language, no reason, no generality or mediation to justify this ultimate responsibility which leads me to absolute sacrifice; absolute sacrifice that is not the sacrifice of irresponsibility on the altar of responsibility, but the sacrifice of the most imperative duty (that which binds me to the other as a singularity in general) in favor of another absolutely imperative duty binding me to every other.

God decides to suspend the sacrificial process, he addresses Abraham who has just said: "Here I am." "Here I am": the first and only possible response to the call by the other, the originary moment of responsibility such as it exposes me to the singular other, the one who appeals to me. "Here I am" is the only self-presentation presumed by every form of responsibility: I am ready to respond, I reply that I am ready to respond. Whereas Abraham has just said "Here I am" and taken his knife to slit his son's throat, God says to him: "Lay not thine hand upon the lad, neither do thou anything unto him: for now I know that thou fearest God, seeing thou hast not withheld thy son, thine only son, from me" (Genesis 22: 12). This terrible declaration seems to display God's satisfaction at the terror that has been expressed (I see that "you fear God [Elohim]," you tremble before me). It causes one to tremble through the fear and trembling it evokes as its only reason (I see that you have trembled before me, all right, we are quits, I free you from your obligation). But it can also be translated or argued as follows: I see that you have understood what absolute

71

duty means, namely, how to respond to the absolute other, to his call, request, or command. These different registers amount to the same thing: by commanding Abraham to sacrifice his son, to put his son to death by offering a gift of death to God, by means of this double gift wherein the gift of death consists in putting to death by raising one's knife over someone and of putting death forward by giving it as an offering, God leaves him free to refuse— and that is the test. The command requests, like a prayer from God, a declaration of love that implores: tell me that you love me, tell me that you turn towards me, towards the unique one, towards the other as unique and, above all, over everything else, unconditionally, and in order to do that, make a gift of death, give death to your only son and give me the death I ask for, that I give to you by asking you for it. In essence God says to Abraham: I can see right away [à l'instant] that you have understood what absolute duty towards the unique one means, that it means responding where there is no reason to be asked for or to be given; I see that not only have you understood that as an idea, but that—and here lies responsibility—you have acted on it, you have put it into effect, you were ready to carry it out *at this very instant* (God stops him *at the very instant when there is no more time, where no more time is given*, it is as if Abraham had *already* killed Isaac: the concept of the instant is always indispensable): thus you had *already* put it into effect, you are absolute responsibility, you had the courage to behave like a murderer in the eyes of the world and of your loved ones, in the eyes of morality, politics, and of the generality of the general or of your kind [*le générique*]. And you had even renounced hope.

Abraham is thus at the same time the most moral and the most immoral, the most responsible and the most irresponsible of men, absolutely irresponsible because he is absolutely responsible, absolutely irresponsible in the face of men and his family, and in the face of the ethical, because he responds absolutely to absolute duty, disinterestedly and without hoping for a reward, without knowing why yet keeping it secret; answering to God and before God. He recognizes neither debt nor duty to his fellows because he is in a relationship to God—a relationship without relation because God is absolutely transcendent, hidden, and secret, not giving any reason he can share in exchange for this doubly given death, not sharing anything in this dissymmetrical alliance. Abraham considers himself to be all square. He acts as if he were discharged of his duty towards his fellows, his son, and humankind; but he continues to love them. He must *love* them and also *owe* them everything in order to be able to sacrifice them. Without being so, then, he nevertheless feels absolved of his duty towards his family, towards the human species [*le genre humain*] and the generality of the ethical, absolved by the absolute of a unique duty that binds him to God the one. Absolute duty absolves him of every debt and releases him from every duty. Absolute ab-solution.

The ideas of secrecy and exclusivity [*non-partage*] are essential here, as is Abraham's silence. He doesn't speak, he doesn't tell his secret to his loved ones. He is, like the knight of faith, a witness and not a teacher (*Fear and Trembling*, 80), and it is true that this witness enters into an absolute relation with the absolute, but he doesn't witness to it in the sense that to witness means to show, teach, illustrate, manifest to others the truth that one can precisely attest to. Abraham is a witness of the absolute faith that cannot and must not witness before men. He must keep his secret. But his silence is not just any silence. Can one witness in silence? By silence?

The tragic hero, on the other hand, can speak, share, weep, complain. He doesn't know "the dreadful responsibility of loneliness" (114). Agamemnon can weep and wail with Clytemnestra and Iphigenia. "Tears and cries are relieving" (114); there is consolation in them. Abraham can neither speak nor commiserate, neither weep nor wail. He is kept in absolute secret. He feels torn, he would like to console the whole world, especially Sarah, Eliezer, and Isaac, he would like to embrace them before taking the final step. But he knows that they will then say to him: "But why are you doing this? Can't you get an exemption, find another solution, discuss, negotiate with God?" Or else they will accuse him of dissimulation and hypocrisy. So he can't say anything to them. Even if he speaks to them he can't say anything to them.

" . . . he speaks no human language. And even if he understood all the languages of the world . . . he still could not speak—he speaks in a divine language, he speaks in tongues" (114). If he were to speak a common or translatable language, if he were to become intelligible by giving his reasons in a convincing manner, he would be giving in to the temptation of the ethical generality that I have referred to as that which makes one irresponsible. He wouldn't be Abraham any more, the unique Abraham in a singular relation with the unique God. Incapable of making a gift of death, incapable of sacrificing what he loved, hence incapable of loving and of hating, he wouldn't give anything anymore.

Abraham says nothing, but his last words, those that respond to Isaac's question, have been recorded: "God himself will provide the lamb for the holocaust, my son." If he had said "There is a lamb, I have one" or "I don't know, I have no idea where to find the lamb," he would have been lying, speaking in order to speak falsehood. By speaking without lying, he responds without responding. This is a strange responsibility that consists neither of responding nor of not responding. Is one responsible for what one says in an unintelligible language, in the language of the other? But besides that, mustn't responsibility always be expressed in a language that is foreign to what the community can already hear or understand only too well? "So he does not speak an untruth, but neither does he say anything, for he is speaking in a strange tongue" (119).

In Melville's "Bartleby the Scrivener," the narrator, a lawyer, cites Job ("with kings and counselors"). Beyond what is a tempting and obvious comparison, the figure of Bartleby could be compared to Job—not to him who hoped to join the kings and counselors one day after his death, but to him who dreamed of not being born. Here, instead of the test God makes Job submit to, one could think of that of Abraham. Just as Abraham doesn't speak a human language, just as he speaks in tongues or in a language that is foreign to every other human language, and in order to do that responds without responding, speaks without saying anything either true or false, says nothing determinate that would be equivalent to a statement, a promise or a lie, in the same way Bartleby's

WHOM TO GIVE TO

"I would prefer not to" takes on the responsibility of a response without response. It evokes the future without either predicting or promising; it utters nothing fixed, determinable, positive, or negative. The modality of this repeated utterance that says nothing, promises nothing, neither refuses or accepts anything, the tense of this singularly insignificant statement reminds one of a nonlanguage or a secret language. Is it not as if Bartleby were also speaking "in tongues"?

But in saying nothing general or determinable, Bartleby doesn't say absolutely nothing. *I would prefer not to* looks like an incomplete sentence. Its indeterminacy creates a tension: it opens onto a sort of reserve of incompleteness; it announces a temporary or provisional reserve, one involving a proviso. Can we not find there the secret of a hypothetical reference to some indecipherable providence or prudence? We don't know what he wants or means to say, or what he doesn't want to do or say, but we are given to understand quite clearly that *he would prefer not to*. The silhouette of a content haunts this response. If Abraham has already consented *to make a gift of death*, and to give to God the death that he is going to put his son to, if he knows that he will do it unless God stops him, can we not say that his disposition is such that he would, precisely, *prefer not to*, without being able to say to the world what is involved? Because he loves his son, he would prefer that God hadn't asked him anything. He would prefer that God didn't let him do it, that he would hold back his hand, that he would provide a lamb for the holocaust, that the moment of this mad decision would lean on the side of nonsacrifice, once the sacrifice were to be accepted. He will not decide *not to*, he has decided *to*, but he would prefer not to. He can say nothing more and will do nothing more if God, if the Other, continues to lead him towards death, to the death that is offered as a gift. And Bartleby's "I would prefer not to" is also a sacrificial passion that will lead him to death, a death given by the law, by a society that doesn't even know why it acts the way it does.

It is difficult not to be struck by the absence of woman in these two monstrous yet banal stories. It is a story of father and son, of masculine figures, of hierarchies among men (God the father,

Abraham, Isaac; the woman, Sarah, is she to whom nothing is said; and Bartleby the Scrivener doesn't make a single allusion to anything feminine whatsoever, even less to anything that could be construed as a figure of woman). Would the logic of sacrificial responsibility within the implacable universality of the law, of its law, be altered, inflected, attenuated, or displaced, if a woman were to intervene in some consequential manner? Does the system of this sacrificial responsibility and of the double "gift of death" imply at its very basis an exclusion or sacrifice of woman? A woman's sacrifice or a sacrifice of woman, according to one sense of the genitive or the other? Let us leave the question in suspense. In the case of the tragic hero or the tragic sacrifice, however, woman is present, her place is central, just as she is present in other tragic works referred to by Kierkegaard.

The responses without response made by Bartleby are at the same time disconcerting, sinister, and comical; superbly, subtly so. There is concentrated in them a sort of sublime irony. Speaking in order not to say anything or to say something other than what one thinks, speaking in such a way as to intrigue, disconcert, question, or have someone or something else speak (the law, the lawyer), means speaking ironically. Irony, in particular Socratic irony, consists of not saying anything, declaring that one doesn't have any knowledge of something, but doing that in order to interrogate, to have someone or something (the lawyer, the law) speak or think. *Eirōneia* dissimulates, it is the act of questioning by feigning ignorance, by pretending. The *I would prefer not to* is not without irony; it cannot not lead one to suppose that there is some irony in the situation. It isn't unlike the incongruous yet familiar humor, the *unheimlich* or uncanniness of the story. On the other hand the author of *The Concept of Irony* uncovers irony in the response without response that translates Abraham's responsibility. Precisely in order to distinguish ironic pretense from a lie, he writes:

> But a final word by Abraham has been preserved, and insofar as I can understand the paradox, I can also understand Abraham's total presence in that word. First and foremost, he does not say anything, and in that form he

says what he has to say. His response to Isaac is in the
form of irony, for it is always irony when I say something
and still do not say anything. (118)

Perhaps irony would permit us to find something like a common
thread in the questions I have just posed and what Hegel said
about woman: that she is "the eternal irony of the community."[5]

Abraham doesn't speak in figures, fables, parables, metaphors,
ellipses, or enigmas. His irony is meta-rhetorical. If he knew what
was going to happen, if for example God had charged him with
the mission of leading Isaac onto the mountain so that He could
strike him with lightning, then he would have been right to have
recourse to enigmatic language. But the problem is precisely that
he doesn't know. Not that that makes him hesitate, however. His
nonknowledge doesn't in any way suspend his own decision,
which remains resolute. The knight of faith must not hesitate.
He accepts his responsibility by heading off towards the absolute
request of the other, beyond knowledge. He decides, but his absolute decision is neither guided nor controlled by knowledge. Such,
in fact, is the paradoxical condition of every decision: it cannot be
deduced from a form of knowledge of which it would simply be
the effect, conclusion, or explicitation. It structurally breaches
knowledge and is thus destined to nonmanifestation; a decision is,
in the end, always secret. It remains secret in the very instant of
its performance, and how can the concept of decision be dissoci-
ated from this figure of the instant? From the stigma of its punc-
tuality?

Abraham's decision is absolutely responsible because it answers
for itself before the absolute other. Paradoxically it is also irresponsible because it is guided neither by reason nor by an ethics justifi-
able before men or before the law of some universal tribunal. Everything points to the fact that one is unable to be responsible at
the same time before the other and before others, before the others
of the other. If God is completely other, the figure or name of the
wholly other, then every other (one) is every (bit) other. *Tout autre*

5. In this regard, I refer the reader to my *Glas* (Lincoln: University of Nebraska
Press, 1986), 190.

est tout autre. This formula disturbs Kierkegaard's discourse on one level while at the same time reinforcing its most extreme ramifications. It implies that God, as the wholly other, is to be found everywhere there is something of the wholly other. And since each of us, everyone else, each other is infinitely other in its absolute singularity, inaccessible, solitary, transcendent, nonmanifest, originarily nonpresent to my *ego* (as Husserl would say of the *alter ego* that can never be originarily present to my consciousness and that I can apprehend only through what he calls *appresentation* and analogy), then what can be said about Abraham's relation to God can be said about my relation without relation to *every other (one) as every (bit) other* [*tout autre comme tout autre*], in particular my relation to my neighbor or my loved ones who are as inaccessible to me, as secret and transcendent as Jahweh. Every other (in the sense of each other) is every bit other (absolutely other). From this point of view what *Fear and Trembling* says about the sacrifice of Isaac is the truth. Translated into this extraordinary story, the truth is shown to possess the very structure of what occurs every day. Through its paradox it speaks of the responsibility required at every moment for every man and every woman. At the same time, there is no longer any ethical generality that does not fall prey to the paradox of Abraham.[6] At the instant of every decision

6. This is the logic of an objection made by Levinas to Kierkegaard: "For Kierkegaard, ethics signifies the general. For him, the singularity of the self would be lost under a rule valid for all; the generality can neither contain nor express the secret of the self. However, it is not at all certain that the ethical is to be found where he looks for it. Ethics as the conscience of a responsibility towards the other . . . does not lose one in the generality, far from it, it singularizes, it posits one as a unique individual, as the Self. . . . In evoking Abraham he describes the meeting with God as occurring where subjectivity is raised to the level of the religious, that is to say above ethics. But one can posit the contrary: the attention Abraham pays to the voice that brings him back to the ethical order by forbidding him to carry out the human sacrifice, is the most intense moment of the drama. . . . It is there, in the ethical, that there is an appeal to the uniqueness of the subject and sense is given to life in defiance of death" (Emmanuel Levinas, *Noms propres* [Montpellier: Fata Morgana, 1976], 113; my translation, DW). Levinas's criticism doesn't prevent him from admiring in Kierkegaard "something absolutely new" in

and through the relation to *every other (one) as every (bit) other*, every one else asks us at every moment to behave like knights of faith. Perhaps that displaces a certain emphasis of Kierkegaard's discourse: the absolute uniqueness of Jahweh doesn't tolerate analogy; we are not all Abrahams, Isaacs, or Sarahs either. We are not Jahweh. But what seems thus to universalize or disseminate the exception or the extraordinary by imposing a supplementary complication upon ethical generality, that very thing ensures that Kierkegaard's text gains added force. It speaks to us of the paradoxical truth of our responsibility and of our relation to the *gift of death* of each instant. Furthermore, it explains to us its own status, namely its ability to be read by all at the very moment when it is speaking to us of secrets in secret, of illegibility and absolute undecipherability. It stands for Jews, Christians, Muslims, but also for everyone else, for every other in its relation to the wholly other. We no longer know who is called Abraham, and he can no longer even tell us.

Whereas the tragic hero is great, admired, and legendary from generation to generation, Abraham, in remaining faithful to his singular love for every other, is never considered a hero. He doesn't make us shed tears and doesn't inspire admiration: rather stupefied horror, a terror that is also secret. For it is a terror that brings us close to the absolute secret, a secret that we share without sharing it, a secret between someone else, Abraham as the other, and another, God as the other, as wholly other. Abraham himself is in secret, cut off both from man and from God.

But that is perhaps what we share with him. But what does it mean to share a secret? It isn't a matter of knowing what the other knows, for Abraham doesn't know anything. It isn't a matter of sharing his faith, for the latter must remain an initiative of absolute singularity. And moreover, we don't think or speak of Abraham from the point of view of a faith that is sure of itself, any more than did Kierkegaard. Kierkegaard keeps coming back to this, re-

---

"European philosophy," "a new modality of the True," "the idea of a persecuted truth" (114–15).

calling that he doesn't understand Abraham, that he wouldn't be capable of doing what he did. Such an attitude in fact seems the only possible one; and even if it is the most widely shared idea in the world, it seems to be required by this monstrosity of such prodigious proportions. Our faith is not assured, because faith can never be, it must never be a certainty. We share with Abraham what cannot be shared, a secret we know nothing about, neither him nor us. To share a secret is not to know or to reveal the secret, it is to share we know not what: nothing that can be determined. What is a secret that is a secret about nothing and a sharing that doesn't share anything?

Such is the secret truth of faith as absolute responsibility and as absolute passion, the "highest passion" as Kierkegaard will say; it is a passion that, sworn to secrecy, cannot be transmitted from generation to generation. In this sense it has no history. This un-transmissibility of the highest passion, the normal condition of a faith which is thus bound to secrecy, nevertheless dictates to us the following: we must always start over. A secret can be transmit-ted, but in transmitting a secret as a secret that remains secret, has one transmitted at all? Does it amount to history, to a story? Yes and no. The epilogue of *Fear and Trembling* repeats, in sentence after sentence, that this highest passion that is faith must be started over by each generation. Each generation must begin again to in-volve itself in it without counting on the generation before. It thus describes the nonhistory of absolute beginnings which are repeated, and the very historicity that presupposes a tradition to be reinvented each step of the way, in this incessant repetition of the absolute beginning.

With *Fear and Trembling*, we hesitate between two generations in the lineage of the so-called religions of the Book: we hesitate at the heart of the Old Testament and of the Jewish religion, but also the heart of a founding event or a key sacrifice for Islam. As for the sacrifice of the son by his father, the son sacrificed by men and finally saved by a God that seemed to have abandoned him or put him to the test, how can we not recognize there the foreshad-owing or the analogy of another passion? As a Christian thinker, Kierkegaard ends by reinscribing the secret of Abraham within a space that seems, in its literality at least, to be evangelical. That doesn't necessarily exclude a Judaic or Islamic reading, but it is a certain evangelical text that seems to orient or dominate Kierkegaard's interpretation. That text isn't cited; rather, like the "kings and counselors" of "Bartleby the Scrivener," it is simply suggested, but this time without the quotation marks, thus being clearly brought to the attention of those who know their texts and have been brought up on the reading of the Gospels:

> But there was no one who could understand Abraham. And yet what did he achieve? He remained true to his love. But anyone who loves God needs no tears, no admiration; he forgets the suffering in the love. Indeed, so completely has he forgotten it that there would not be the slightest trace of his suffering left if God himself did not remember it, *for he sees in secret* and recognizes distress and counts the tears and forgets nothing.
>
> Thus, either there is a paradox, that the single individual stands in an absolute relation to the absolute, or Abraham is lost. (120, my emphasis)

FOUR

Tout Autre Est Tout Autre

The danger is so great that I excuse the suppression of the object.
BAUDELAIRE, "The Pagan School"

. . . that stroke of genius called Christianity.
NIETZSCHE, *The Genealogy of Morals*

"Every other (one) is every (bit) other"—the stakes seem to be altered by the trembling of this dictum. It is no doubt too economical, too elliptical, and hence, like any formula so isolated and capable of being transmitted out of its context, too close to the coded language of a password. One uses it to play with the rules, to cut someone or something short, to aggressively circumscribe a domain of discourse. It becomes the secret of all secrets. Is it not sufficient to transform what one complacently calls a context in order to demystify the shibboleth or decipher all the secrets of the world?

Is not this dictum—*tout autre est tout autre*—in the first place a tautology? It doesn't signify anything that one doesn't already know, if by that one simply refers to the repetition of a subject in its complement and if by so doing one avoids bringing to bear upon it an interpretation that would distinguish between the two homonyms *tout* and *tout*, an indefinite pronominal adjective (some, someone, some other one) and an adverb of quantity (totally, absolutely, radically, infinitely other). But once one appeals to the supplement of a contextual sign in order to mark a distinction between the two grammatical functions and the two senses of what appears to be the same word—*tout*—then one must also distinguish between the two *autres*. If the first *tout* is an indefinite pronominal adjective, then the first *autre* becomes a noun and the second, in all probability, an adjective or attribute. One no longer has a case of tautology but instead a radical heterology; indeed this introduces the principle of the most irreducible heterology. Or else, as a further alternative, one might consider that in both cases (tautology and heterology, with or without the homonym) the two *autres* are repeated in the monotony of a tautology that wins out after all, the monotony of a principle of identity that, thanks to the copula and sense of being, would here take over alterity itself, nothing less than that, in order to say: the other is the other, that is always so, the alterity of the other is the alterity of the other. And the secret of that formula would close upon a hetero-tautological speculation that always risks meaning nothing. But we know from experience that the speculative always requires a hetero-tautological position. That is its definition according to Hegel's speculative idealism, and it is the impetus for the dialectic within the horizon of absolute knowledge. The hetero-tautological position introduces the law of speculation, and of speculation on every secret.

We are not just playing here, turning this little sentence around in order to make it dazzle from every angle. We would only pay slight and bemused attention to this particular formula and to the form of this key if, in the discreet displacement that affects the functions of the two words there didn't appear, as if on the same musical scale, two alarmingly different themes [*partitions*, (musical) scores] that, through their disturbing likeness, emerge as incompatible.

One of them keeps in reserve the possibility of reserving the quality of the wholly other, in other words the *infinite other*, for God alone, or in any case for a single other. The other attributes to or recognizes in this infinite alterity of the wholly other, every other, in other words each, each one, for example each man and woman. Even in its critique of Kierkegaard concerning ethics and generality Levinas's thinking stays within the game—the play of difference and analogy—between the face of God and the face of my neighbor, between the infinitely other as God and the infinitely other as another human.[1] If every human is wholly other, if everyone else, or every other one, is every bit other, then one can no longer distinguish between a claimed generality of ethics that would need to be sacrificed in sacrifice, and the faith that turns towards God alone, as wholly other, turning away from human duty. But since Levinas also wants to distinguish between the infinite alterity of God and the "same" infinite alterity of every human, or of the other in general, then he cannot simply be said to be saying something different from Kierkegaard. Neither one nor the other can assure himself of a concept of the ethical and of the religious that is of consequence; and consequently they are especially unable to determine the limit between those two orders. Kierkegaard would have to admit, as Levinas reminds him, that ethics is also the order of and respect for absolute singularity, and not only that of the generality or of the repetition of the same. He cannot therefore distinguish so conveniently between the ethical and the religious. But for his part, in taking into account absolute singularity, that is, the absolute alterity obtaining in relations between one human and another, Levinas is no longer able to distinguish between the infinite alterity of God and that of every human. His ethics is already a religious one. In the two cases the border between the ethical and the religious becomes more than problematic, as do all attendant discourses.

This applies all the more to political or legal matters. The concept of responsibility, like that of decision, would thus be found to lack coherence or consequence, even lacking identity with respect to itself, paralyzed by what can be called an aporia or an antimony. That has never stopped it from "functioning," as one says. On the contrary, it operates so much better, to the extent that it serves to obscure the abyss or fill in its absence of foundation, stabilizing a chaotic process of change in what are called conventions. Chaos refers precisely to the abyss or the open mouth, that which speaks as well as that which signifies hunger.

---

1. Cf. note 6, p. 78, and "Violence and Metaphysics," in Derrida, *Writing and Difference*, trans. Alan Bass (Chicago: University of Chicago Press, 1978), 96, 110ff.

What is thus found at work in everyday discourse, in the exercise of justice, and first and foremost in the axiomatics of private, public, or international law, in the conduct of internal politics, diplomacy, and war, is a lexicon concerning responsibility that can be said to hover vaguely about a concept that is nowhere to be found, even if we can't go so far as to say that it doesn't correspond to any concept at all. It amounts to a disavowal whose resources, as one knows, are inexhaustible. One simply keeps on denying the aporia and antimony, tirelessly, and one treats as nihilist, relativist, even poststructuralist, and worse still deconstructionist, all those who remain concerned in the face of such a display of good conscience.

The sacrifice of Isaac is an abomination in the eyes of all, and it should continue to be seen for what it is—atrocious, criminal, unforgivable; Kierkegaard insists on that. The ethical point of view must remain valid: Abraham is a murderer. However, is it not true that the spectacle of this murder, which seems intolerable in the denseness and rhythm of its theatricality, is at the same time the most common event in the world? Is it not inscribed in the structure of our existence to the extent of no longer constituting an event? It will be said that it would be most improbable for the sacrifice of Isaac to be repeated in our day; and it certainly seems that way. We can hardly imagine a father taking his son to be sacrificed on the top of the hill at Montmartre. If God didn't send a lamb as a substitute or an angel to hold back his arm, there would still be a prosecutor, preferably with expertise in Middle Eastern violence, to accuse him of infanticide or first-degree murder; and if a psychiatrist who was both something of a psychoanalyst and something of a journalist declared that the father was "responsible," carrying on as if psychoanalysis had done nothing to upset the order of discourse on intention, conscience, good will, etc., the criminal father would have no chance of getting away with it. He might claim that the wholly other had ordered him to do it, and perhaps in secret (how would he know that?), in order to test his faith, but it would make no difference. Things are such that this man would surely be condemned by any civilized society. On the other hand, the smooth functioning of such a society, the monotonous complacency of its discourses on morality, politics, and the law, and the exercise of its rights (whether public, private, national or international), are in no way impaired by the fact that, because of the structure of the laws of the market that society has instituted and controls, because of the mechanisms of external debt and other similar inequities, that same "society" *puts to* death or (but failing to help someone in distress accounts for only a minor difference) *allows* to die of hunger and disease tens of millions of children (those neighbors or fellow humans that ethics or the discourse of the rights of man refer to) without any moral or legal tribunal ever being considered competent to judge such a sacrifice, the sacrifice of others to avoid being sacrificed oneself. Not only is it true that such a society participates in this incalculable sacrifice, it actually organizes it. The smooth functioning of its economic, political, and legal affairs, the smooth functioning of its moral discourse and good conscience presupposes the permanent operation of this sacrifice. And such a sacrifice is not even invisible, for from time to time television shows us, while keeping them at a distance, a series of intolerable images, and a few voices are raised to bring it all to our attention. But those images and voices are completely powerless to induce the slightest effective change in the situation, to assign the least responsibility, to furnish anything more than a convenient alibi. That this order is founded upon a bottomless chaos (the abyss or open mouth) is something that will necessarily be brought home one day to those who just as necessarily forget the same. We are not even talking about wars, the less recent or most recent ones, in which cases one can wait an eternity for morality or international law (whether violated with impunity or invoked hypocritically) to determine with any degree of certainty who is responsible or guilty for the hundreds of thousands of victims who are sacrificed for what or whom one knows not, countless victims, each of whose singularity becomes each time infinitely singular, every other (one) being every (bit) other, whether they be victims of the Iraqi state or victims of the international coalition that accuses the latter of not respecting the law. For in the discourses that dominate during such wars, it is rigorously impossible, on one side and the other, to discern the religious from the moral, the legal from the political. The warring factions are all irreconcilable fellow worshipers of the religions of the Book. Does that not make things converge once again in the fight to the death that continues to rage on Mount Moriah over the possession of the secret of the sacrifice by an Abraham who never said anything? Do they not fight in order to take possession of the secret as the sign of an alliance with God and to impose its order on the other, who becomes for his part nothing more than a murderer?

The trembling of the formula "every other (one) is every (bit) other" can also be reproduced. It can do so to the extent of replacing one of the "every others" by God: "Every other (one) is God," or "God is every (bit) other." Such a substitution in no way alters the "extent" of the original formulation, whatever grammatical function be assigned to the various words. In one case God is defined as infinitely other, as wholly other, every bit other. In the other case it is declared that every other one, each of the others, is God inasmuch as he or she is, *like* God, wholly other.

Are we just playing here? If this were a game, then it would need to be kept safe and untouched, like the game that must be kept alive between humans and God. For the game between these two unique "every others," like the same "every other," opens the space and introduces the hope of salvation, the economy of "saving oneself" that we shall shortly discuss. Linking alterity to singularity or to what one could call the universal exception or the law of the exception (*tout autre est tout autre* signifies that every other is singular, that every one is a singularity, which also means that every one is each one, a proposition that seals the contract between universality and the exception of singularity), this play of words seems to contain the very possibility of a secret that hides and reveals itself at the same time within a single sentence and, more than that, within a single language. Or at least within a finite group of languages, within the finitude of language as that which opens onto the infinite. The essential and abyssal equivocality, that is, the play of the several senses of *tout autre est tout autre* or *Dieu est tout autre*, is not, in its literality (that of French or Italian, for example), universally translatable according to a traditional concept of translation. The sense of the play can no doubt be translated by a paraphrase in other languages; but not the formal economy of the slippage between two homonyms in the language that can here be called singularly my own, that is, the use of *tout* as indefinite pronominal adjective and as an adverb, and *autre* as indefinite pronominal adjective and noun. We have here a kind of *shibboleth*, a secret formula such as can be uttered only in a certain way in a certain language. As a chance or aleatory effect, the untranslatability of this formal economy functions like a secret within one's so-called natural or mother tongue. One can regret such a limiting function or on the contrary take pride in it; one can derive some national prestige from it but either way there is nothing to be done or said about such a secret of the mother tongue. It is there before us in its possibility, the *Geheimnis* of language that ties it to the home, to the motherland, to the birth-place, to economy, to the law of the *oikos*, in short to the family and to the family of words derived from *heim*—home, *heimlich*, *unheimlich*, *Geheimnis*, etc.

What might this secret of the mother tongue have to do with the secret that the father sees in, as the Gospel according to Matthew puts it, and that Kierkegaard refers to at the end of *Fear and Trembling?* There is a secret of the mother tongue, the secret that the father's lucidity sees in, and the secret of the sacrifice of Isaac. It is indeed an economy, literally a matter of the law (*nomos*) of the home (*oikos*), of the family and of the hearth [*foyer*, hearth, focus]; and of the space separating or associating the fire of the family hearth and the fire of the sacrificial holocaust. A double foyer, focus, or hearth, a double fire and double light; two ways of loving, burning, and seeing.

To see in secret—what can that mean?

Before recognizing there a quote from the Gospel according to Matthew (*videre in abscondito / en tō kryptō blepein*) let us note that the penetration of the secret is entrusted to the gaze, to sight, to observation, rather than to hearing, smelling, or touching. One might imagine a secret that could only be penetrated or traversed, undone or opened as a secret, by hearing, or one that would only allow itself to be touched or felt, precisely because in that way it would escape the gaze or be invisible, or indeed because what was visible in it would keep secret the secret that wasn't visible. One can always reveal to the gaze something that still remains secret because its secret is accessible only to senses other than sight. For example, there might be some writing that I can't decipher (a letter in Chinese or Hebrew, or simply some undecipherable handwriting) but that remains perfectly visible in spite of its being sealed to most readers. It isn't hidden but it is encoded or encrypted. That which is hidden, as that which remains inaccessible to the eye or the hand, is not necessarily encrypted in the derivative senses of that word—ciphered, coded, to be interpreted—in contrast to being hidden in the shadows (which is what it also meant in Greek).

What should we make of the slight difference that appears in the Gospel between the Greek and the Latin of the Vulgate? In *in abscondito, absconditus* refers rather to the hidden, the secret, the mysterious as that which retreats into the invisible, that which is lost from sight. The majority of examples or figures on the basis of which *absconditus* has come to mean secrecy in general, and so has become synonymous with *secretum* (separate, retired, withdrawn from view), privilege the optical dimension. The absolute sense of what withdraws from view is not necessarily, of course, that of a visible that conceals itself, for example, my hand under the table—my hand is visible as such but I can render it invisible. The absolute sense of invisibility resides rather in the idea of that which has no structure of visibility, for example, the voice, what is said or meant, and sound. Music is not invisible in the same way as a veiled sculpture. The voice is not invisible in the same way as skin under clothing. The nudity of a timbre or a whisper doesn't have the same quality as the nudity of a man's or woman's breast; it signifies neither the same nudity nor the same modesty. In contrast to *absconditus* (not to mention *mystique*), the Greek lexicon referring to the cryptic (*kryptō, kryptos, kryptikōs, kryphios, kryphaiōs*, etc.), while of course also referring to the concealed, dissimulated, secret, clandestine, etc., seems on the other hand to delineate a stricter sense, one less manifest to sight one might say. It extends beyond the visible. And in this semantic history, the cryptic has come to enlarge the field of secrecy beyond the nonvisible towards whatever resists deciphering, the secret as illegible or undecipherable rather than invisible.

Nevertheless, that the two senses communicate so easily, that they can be translated one within the other or one into the other, is perhaps attributable to the fact, among others, that the in-visible can be understood, it might be said, in *two ways*.

1. There is a visible in-visible, an invisible of the order of the visible that I can keep in secret by keeping it out of sight. This invisible can be artificially kept from sight while remaining within what one can call exteriority (if I hide a nuclear arsenal in underground silos or hide explosives in a cache, there is a visible surface involved; and if I hide a part of my body under clothes or a veil, it is a matter of concealing one surface beneath another; whatever one conceals in this way becomes invisible but remains within the order of visibility; it remains constitutively visible. In the same way but according to a different structure, what one calls the interior organs of the body—my heart, my kidneys, my blood, my brain—are naturally said to be invisible, but they are still of the order of visibility: an operation or accident can expose them or bring them to the surface; their interiority is provisional and bringing their invisibility into view is something that can be proposed or promised). All that is of the order of the visible in-visible.

2. But there is also absolute invisibility, the absolutely non-visible that refers to whatever falls outside of the register of sight, namely, the sonorous, the musical, the vocal or phonic (and hence the phonological or discursive in the strict sense), but also the tactile and odoriferous. And desire, like curiosity, like the experience of modesty [*pudeur*] and the unveiling of secrecy, the revealing of the *pudenda* or the fact of "seeing in secret," all those movements that take secrecy beyond the secret necessarily come into play. But they can come into play only within these limits ascribed to the invisible: the invisible as concealed visible, the encrypted invisible or the non-visible as that which is other than visible. This is an immense problem that appears both classic and enigmatic yet each time as if new, and we can merely draw attention to it here. When Kierkegaard-de Silentio makes a barely veiled reference to the Gospel of Matthew, the allusion to "your father who sees in

secret (*qui videt in abscondito / ho blepōn en tō kryptō*)" echoes across the reach of these limits.

In the first place the allusion describes a relation to the wholly other, hence an absolute dissymmetry. It is all that suffices to provoke the *mysterium tremendum*, inscribing itself within the order of the gaze. God sees me, he looks into me in secret, but I don't see him, I don't see him looking at me, even though he looks at me while facing me and not, like an analyst, from behind my back. Since I don't see him looking at me, I can, and must, only hear him. But most often I have to be led to hear or believe him [*on doit me le donner à entendre*], I hear tell what he says, through the voice of another, another other, a messenger, an angel, a prophet, a messiah or postman [*facteur*], a bearer of tidings, an evangelist, an intermediary who speaks between God and myself. There is no face-to-face exchange of looks between God and myself, between the other and myself. God looks at me and I don't see him and it is on the basis of this gaze that singles me out [*ce regard qui me regarde*] that my responsibility comes into being. Thus is instituted or revealed the "it concerns me" or "it's my lookout" [*ça me regarde*] that leads me to say "it is my business, my affair, my responsibility." But not in the sense of a (Kantian) autonomy by means of which I see myself acting in total liberty or according to a law that I make for myself, rather in the heteronomy of an "it's my lookout" even when I can't see anything and can take no initiative, there where I cannot preempt by my own initiative whatever is commanding me to make decisions, decisions that will nevertheless be mine and which I alone will have to answer for.

It is dissymmetrical: this gaze that sees me without my seeing it looking at me. It knows my very secret even when I myself don't see it and even though the Socratic "Know yourself" seems to install the philosophical within the lure of reflexivity, in the disavowal of a secret that is always *for me alone*, that is to say *for the other*: *for me* who never sees anything in it, and hence *for the other* alone to whom, through the dissymmetry, a secret is revealed. For the other my secret will no longer be a secret. The two uses of "for" don't have the same sense: at least in this case the secret that is for me is what I can't see; the secret that is for the other is

FOUR

what is revealed only to the other, that she alone can see. By
disavowing this secret, philosophy would have come to reside in
a misunderstanding of what there is to know, namely, that there
is secrecy and that it is incommensurable with knowing, with
knowledge and with objectivity, as in the incommensurable "subjective interiority" that Kierkegaard extracts from every knowledge
relation of the subject/object type.

How can another see into me, into my most secret self, without
my being able to see in there myself and without my being able
to see him in me? And if my secret self, that which can be revealed
only to the other, to the wholly other, to God if you wish, is a
secret that I will never reflect on, that I will never know or experience or possess as my own, then what sense is there in saying that
it is "my" secret, or in saying more generally that a secret *belongs*,
that it is proper to or belongs to some "one," or to some *other* who
remains some*one?* It is perhaps there that we find the secret of
secrecy, namely, that it is not a matter of knowing and that it is
there for no-one. A secret doesn't belong, it can never be said to
be at home or in its place [*chez soi*]. Such is the *Unheimlichkeit* of
the *Geheimnis*, and we need to systematically question the reach of
this concept as it functions, in a regulated manner, in two systems
of thought that extend equally, although in different ways, beyond
an axiomatic of the self or the *chez soi* as *ego cogito*, as consciousness
or representative intentionality, for example, and in an exemplary
fashion in Freud and Heidegger.[2] The question of the self: "who
am I?" not in the sense of "who am I" but "who is this 'I'" that
can say "who"? What is the "I," and what becomes of responsibility once the identity of the "I" trembles *in secret?*

This dissymmetry of the gaze leads us back to what Patočka
suggests concerning sacrifice and concerning the tradition of the
mysterium tremendum. In spite of the opposition that seems to obtain
between *Fear and Trembling* and the Kantian logic of autonomy,
Kierkegaard still follows the Kantian tradition of a pure ethics or
practical reason that is exceeded by absolute duty as it extends

2. This task can only be outlined here. It is the subject of the seminar referred
to in note 5, p. 10.

into the realm of sacrifice. Access to pure duty is, in Kant's terms, also "sacrifice," the sacrifice of the passions, of the affections, of so-called "pathological" interests; everything that links my sensibility to the empirical world, to calculation, and to the conditionality of hypothetical imperatives. The unconditionality of respect for the law also dictates a sacrifice (*Aufopferung*) which is always a sacrifice of self (even for Abraham when he gets ready to kill his son; he inflicts the most severe suffering upon himself, he gives to himself the death that he is granting his son and also giving, in another way, to God; he puts his son to death or grants him death and offers the death so given to God). According to Kant the unconditionality of moral law dictates the violence that is exercised in self-restraint (*Selbstzwang*) and against one's own desires, interests, affections, or drives. But one is driven to sacrifice by a sort of practical drive, by a form of motivation that is also instinctive, but an instinct that is pure and practical, respect for moral law being its sensible manifestation. The *Critique of Practical Reason* (Chapter 3, "Of the Motives of Pure Practical Reason") closely links the *Aufopferung*, sacrifice of self and obligation, to debt and duty, which are never separable from guilt (*Schuldigkeit*), from that which one never catches up with, that which one can never acquit oneself of or settle.

Patočka describes the coming of Christian subjectivity and the repression of Platonism through recourse to a *figure* [*figure*, also "face"], one might say, that inscribes sacrifice within the dissymmetry of looks that cannot be exchanged. He does so literally on at least two occasions: "*Tremendum*, because responsibility resides henceforth not in an essence that is accessible to the human gaze, that of the Good and the One, but in the relation to a supreme, absolute and inaccessible being that holds us in check not by exterior but interior force" (116). This is the moment where the light or sun of the Good, as invisible source of intelligible visibility, but which is not itself an eye, goes beyond philosophy to become, in the Christian faith, a gaze. A personal gaze, that is, a face, a figure, and not a sun. The Good becomes personal Goodness, a gaze that sees me without my seeing it. A little later there is this "suppression of the object," as Baudelaire might have put it: "In the final analysis the soul is not a relation to an *object*, however elevated (such as the Platonic Good), but to a person who fixes it in his gaze while at the same time remaining beyond the reach of the gaze of that soul. As for knowing what this person is, such a question has not yet received an adequate thematic development within the perspective of Christianity" (ibid.).

This look that cannot be exchanged is what situates originary culpability and original sin; it is the essence of responsibility. But at the same time it sets in train the search for salvation through sacrifice. The word "sacrifice" is used a little further on, in the context of Judeo-Christian history (Patočka's single reference to the Old Testament) and of the being-towards-death, of what we are here calling the apprehension of the gift of death, or death as an offering:

> . . . an opening onto the abyssality of divinity and of humanity, of a theanthropy that is utterly unique and, for this reason, decisive in a most definitive manner. The essential content of the soul derives entirely from this drama without precedent. The classically transcendent God, combined with the Lord of the Old Testament story, becomes the principal character in this interior play around which he creates the drama of redemption and grace. The surpassing of the everyday takes the form of concern for salvation of the soul, the latter being conquered by means of a moral transformation, by means of a reversal in the face of death and of eternal death, living in anguish and hope that couldn't be more closely allied one with the other, trembling in the consciousness of sin and offering one's whole being in the sacrifice of repentance." (117)

As we were saying earlier, a *general economy of sacrifice* could be deployed according to several forms of "logic" or "calculation." From the point of view of their limits, calculation, logic, and even economy in the strict sense point precisely to what is at stake or what

is suspended or *epochalized* in such an *economy of sacrifice.*[3] Through
their differences these economies perhaps perform decipherings of
what is one and the *same* economy. But "amounting to the same
thing," like economy, could also be an inexhaustible operation.

At the moment when Kierkegaard concludes by re-
Christianizing or pre-Christianizing the sacrifice of Isaac with such
determination, as if he were *preparing the way* for Christianity, he
implicitly refers to the Gospel of Matthew: "For he (God the Father) sees in secret and recognizes distress and counts the tears
and forgets nothing" (*Fear and Trembling*, 120). God sees in secret,
he knows. But it is as if he didn't know what Abraham was going
to do, or decide, or decide to do. He gives him back his son after
assuring himself that Abraham has trembled, renounced all hope,
and irrevocably decided to sacrifice his beloved son to him. Abraham had consented to suffer death or worse, and that without
calculating, without investing, beyond any perspective of recoup-
ing the loss; hence, it seems, beyond recompense or retribution,
beyond economy, without any hope of remuneration [*salaire*]. The
sacrifice of economy, that without which there is no free responsibility or decision (a decision always takes place beyond calculation), is indeed in this case the sacrifice of the *oikonomia*, namely
of the law of the home (*oikos*), of the hearth, of what is one's own
or proper, of the private, of the love and affection of one's kin.
This is the moment when Abraham gives the sign of absolute
sacrifice, namely, by putting to death or giving death to his own,
putting to death his absolute love for what is dearest, the only son;
this is the instant in which the sacrifice is as it were consummated,
for only an instant, a *no-time-lapse*, separates this from the raised
arm of the murderer himself; this is the impossible to grasp instant
of absolute imminence in which Abraham can no longer go back
on his decision, nor even suspend it. *In this instant*, therefore, in

3. Concerning this economy of sacrifice, I refer the reader once again to *Glas*,
notably 32-33, 41ff. (on Hegel, Abraham, the "sacrifice" of Isaac and the "economic
simulacrum"), 68ff., 96, 108, 119, 123, 139-41, 155ff., 207-8, 235, 240-43, 253ff.,
259ff.; and to "Economimesis," trans. Richard Klein, *Diacritics* 11, 2 (1981).

the imminence that doesn't even separate the decision from the act, God returns his son to him and decides by sovereign decision, by an absolute gift, to reinscribe sacrifice within an economy by means of what thenceforth comes to resemble a reward.

On the basis of the Gospel of Matthew we can ask what "to give back" or "to pay back" means ("thy Father which seeth in secret shall reward thee [*reddet tibi / apodōsei soi*]").[4] God decides to *give back*, to give back life, to give back the beloved son, once he is assured that a gift outside of any economy, the gift of death—and of the death of that which is priceless—has been accomplished without any hope of exchange, reward, circulation, or communication. To speak of the secret between God and Abraham is to also say that, in order that there be this gift as sacrifice, all communication between them has to be suspended, whether that be communication as an exchange of words, signs, or promises, or communication as exchange of goods, of things, of riches or property. Abraham renounces all sense and all property—that is where the responsibility of absolute duty begins. Abraham is in a position of nonexchange with respect to God, he is in secret since he doesn't speak to God and expects neither response nor reward from him. The response and hence responsibility always risk what they cannot avoid appealing to in reply [*en retour*], namely, recompense and retribution. They risk the exchange that they might expect but are at the same time unable to count on.

It is finally in renouncing life, the life of his son that one has every reason to think is as precious as his own, that Abraham gains or wins. He risks winning; more precisely, having renounced winning, expecting neither response nor recompense, expecting nothing that can be *given back* to him, nothing that will *come back* to him (when we once defined dissemination as "that which doesn't come back to the father" we might as well have been describing the instant of Abraham's renunciation), he sees that God gives back to him, in the instant of absolute renunciation, the very thing

4. The French translates the Latin and Greek more literally than the English as *(il) te le rendra* ("he will give it back to you" or "he will pay you back").—Trans. note.

that he had already, in the same instant, decided to sacrifice. It is given back to him because he renounced calculation. Demystifiers of this superior or sovereign calculation that consists in no more calculating might say that he played his cards well. Through the law of the father economy reappropriates the *an*economy of the gift as a gift of life or, what amounts to the same thing, a gift of death.

Let us come back to Matthew (Chap. 6). On three occasions there returns this truth, like some obsessive reminder to be learned by heart. It is the sentence "and thy Father which seeth in secret shall reward thee (*reddet tibi / apodōsei soi*)." It is a truth "to be learned by heart" in the first place because one has the impression of having to learn it without understanding it, like a repeated and repeatable formula (like our *tout autre est tout autre* just now, a sort of obscure proverb that one can transmit and transport without understanding it, like a sealed message that can be passed from hand to hand or whispered from mouth to ear). It is a matter of learning "by heart" beyond any semantic comprehension. In fact God asks that one give without knowing, without calculating, reckoning, or hoping, for one must give without counting, and that is what takes it outside of sense. But we say "to be learned by heart" for another reason. This passage is also a meditation or sermon on the heart, on what the heart is and more precisely what it *should be* should it return to its rightful place. The essence of the heart, that is, there where the heart is what it must properly be, there where it properly takes place, in its correct *location*, that is the very thing that gives us food for thought concerning economy. For the place of the heart is, or rather is called or destined to be, the place of true riches, a place of treasures, the placement of the greatest *thesaurization* or laying up of treasures. The correct location of the heart is the place that is best placed.

This passage from the Gospels turns, as we know, on the question of justice, and especially what we might call economic justice: alms-giving, wages, debt, laying up of treasures. Now the line demarcating celestial from terrestrial economy is what allows one to situate the rightful place of the heart. One must not lay up treasures for oneself on earth but in heaven. After saying for the

third time, here on the mountain, "and thy Father which seeth in
secret shall reward thee" (in other words "you can count on the
economy of heaven if you sacrifice the earthly economy"), Jesus
teaches as follows:

> Lay not up for yourselves treasures upon earth (*Nolite
> thesaurizare vobis thesauros in terra*), where moth and rust
> doth corrupt, and where thieves break through and steal.
> But lay up for yourselves treasures in heaven (*Thesaurizate
> autem vobis thesauros in caelo*), where neither moth nor rust
> doth corrupt, and where thieves do not break through and
> steal. For where treasure is, there will your heart be also
> (*Ubi enim est thesaurus tuus, ibi est cor tuum / hopou gar estin
> thesauros sou, ekei estai kai he kardia sou*). (Matthew 6: 19-21)

Where is the heart? What is the heart? The heart will thus be,
in the future, wherever you save real treasure, that which is not
visible on earth, that whose capital accumulates beyond the economy of the terrestrial visible or sensible, that is, the corrupted or
corruptible economy that is vulnerable to moth, rust, and thieves.
That does more than imply the pricelessness of celestial capital. It
is invisible. It doesn't devalue, it can never be stolen from you.
The celestial coffers are more secure, unbreakable, out of reach of
any forced entry or ill-conceived gamble on the market. This capital that cannot be devalued will yield an infinite profit, it is an
infinitely secure placement, better than the best, a chattel without
price.

As a discourse on the location or placement of the heart this
cardiotopology is also an ophthalmology. The celestial treasure is
invisible to the eyes of corrupted and corruptible flesh. There is
the good and simple eye (*oculus simplex / ophthalmos haplous*), and
the bad, corrupt, or depraved eye (*nequam/poneros*):

> The light of the body is the eye (*Lucerna corporis tui est
> oculus tuus / Ho lukhnos tou somatos estin ho ophthalmos*): if
> therefore thine eye be single (*simplex/haplous*—the Gros-
> jean and Léturmy French translation gives "healthy"
> [*sain*]), thy whole body shall be full of light. But if thine

eye be evil, thy whole body shall be full of darkness. If
therefore the light that is in thee be darkness, how great
is that darkness. (Matthew 6: 22-23)

The organ of sight begins by being a source of light. The eye
is a lamp. It doesn't receive light, it gives it. It is not that which
receives or regards the Good on the outside as solar source of
visibility, it gives light from the inside. It is therefore the Good
become goodness, the becoming-good of the Good, since it lights
from the interior, from the inside of the body, namely, the soul.
However, although it is internal in its source, this light doesn't
belong to this world or this earth. It can seem obscure, somber,
nocturnal, secret, invisible to eyes of flesh, to corrupted eyes, and
that is why "seeing in secret" becomes necessary. In this way God
the Father reestablishes an economy that was interrupted by the
dividing of earth and heaven.

This passage from the Gospel of Matthew deals, if it can be
put thus, with justice, with what it is to be just or to do justly
(*justitiam facere / dikaiosynēn poiein*). Jesus had praised the poor in
spirit (*pauperes spiritu / ptōkhoi tō pneumati:* beggars in spirit). The
sermon is organized around the question of poverty, begging,
alms, and charity, of what it means to *give for Christ*, of what
giving means *to Christ*, and what it means to give *for Christ*, to him,
in his name, for him, in a new fraternity with him and on his
terms, as well as what it means to be just in so giving, for, in, and
according to Christ. The kingdom of heaven is promised to the
poor in spirit who are blessed, elated [*dans l'allégresse*] (*beati/ma-
karioi*), along with they that mourn, the meek, they which do
hunger and thirst after righteousness, the merciful, the pure in
heart, the peacemakers, they which are persecuted for righteousness' sake, those reviled for God's sake. All those are promised
remuneration, a reward, a token (*merces/misthos*), a good salary, a
great reward (*merces copiosa / misthos polus*), *in heaven*. It is thus that
the real heavenly treasure is constituted, on the basis of the salary
or price paid for sacrifice or renunciation on earth, and more precisely on the basis of the price paid to those who have been able
to raise themselves above the earthly or literal justice of the Scribes

and Pharisees, the men of letters, of the body and of the earth. If
your justice does not exceed that of the Scribes and Pharisees or
the men of letters, as opposed to those of the spirit, you will not
enter the kingdom of heaven. One can translate that as follows:
you won't receive your wages (*mercedem*).

A *logic* is thus put in place. One can note certain of its character-
istics.

A. *On the one hand*, we have here a *photology* in terms of which
the source of light comes from the heart, from inside; from the
spirit and not from the world. After saying "Ye are the salt of the
earth," Christ says in the same movement "Ye are the light of
the world (*lux mundi / phōs tou kosmou*)," and "A city that is set on
an hill cannot be hid (*abscondi/krybenai*)" (Matthew 5: 14). A mutation takes place in the history of secrecy. If the light was in the
world, if it had its source outside and not within us, within the
spirit, one would be able to conceal objects, cities, nuclear arms.
The object wouldn't disappear but be hidden behind a screen.
Only an apparatus of this world would be required to create secret
places. A *thing* would be hidden by another, sheltered behind or
beneath *something;* apparatuses, caches, or crypts would be constructed and the secret would be kept invisible. But once the light
is in us, within the interiority of the spirit, then secrecy is no
longer possible. This sort of omnipresence is more radical, effective, and undeniable than that of a spy satellite that turns, as one
says, "in space." Nothing sensible or terrestrial would be able to
stand in its way. There would be no obstacle to interrupt the
gaze.

The interiorization of the photological source marks the end of
secrecy but it is also the beginning of the paradox of the secret as
irreducible in its interiority. No more secrecy means more secrecy
[*plus de secret, plus de secret*]: that is another secret of secrecy, another
formula or *shibboleth* that depends entirely on whether or not you
pronounce the final *s* of *plus*, a distinction that cannot be seen
literally.⁵ There where, wherever, or, since place no longer takes place

5. The final *s* of *plus* is pronounced in the expression *plus de secret* to mean
"more secret(s)/secrecy" and not pronounced when it means "no more secret(s)/
secrecy."—Trans. note.

one should say more precisely *as soon as* there is no longer any secret hidden from God or from the spiritual light that passes through every space, then a recess of spiritual subjectivity and of absolute interiority is constituted allowing secrecy to be formed within it. Subtracted from space, this incommensurable inside of the soul or the conscience, this inside without any outside carries with it both the end and the origin of the secret. *Plus de secret.* For if there were no absolutely heterogeneous interiority separate from objectivity, if there were no inside that could not be objectified, there would be no secrecy either. Whence the strange economy of the secret as economy *of* sacrifice that is brought to bear here. And again, there is an instability in the grammatical play of the genitive in this expression or formula "economy of sacrifice": one economizes thanks to sacrifice and one economizes sacrifice; it is a sacrifice that economizes or an economy that sacrifices.

B. *On the other hand*, if this spiritualization of the "interior" light institutes a new economy (an economy of sacrifice: you will receive good wages if you rise above earthly gain, you will get a better salary if you give up your earthly salary, one salary is waged against another), then it is by breaking with, dissociating from, or rendering dissymmetrical whatever is paired with the sensible body, in the same way that it means breaking with exchange as a simple form of reciprocity. In the same way, so as not to reinscribe alms-giving within a certain economy of exchange, he will say "But when thou doest alms, let not thy left hand know what thy right hand doeth" (6: 3), so "if thy right eye offend thee [*te scandalise*], pluck it out, and cast it from thee" (5: 29). Similarly for the hand:

> Ye have heard that it was said by them of old time, Thou shalt not commit adultery: But I say unto you, That whosoever looketh on a woman to lust after her hath committed adultery with her already in his heart.
> And if thy right eye offend (*scandalizat/skandalizei*: the *skandalon* is what makes one fall, stumble, sin) thee, pluck it out, and cast it far from thee: for it is profitable for thee that one of thy members should perish, and not that thy

whole body should be cast into hell. And if thy right hand offend thee, cut it off, and cast it from thee: for it is profitable for thee that one of thy members should perish, and not that thy whole body should be cast into hell. (Matthew 5: 27-30)

Such an economic calculation integrates absolute loss. It breaks with exchange, symmetry, or reciprocity. It is true that absolute subjectivity has brought with it calculation and a limitless raising of the stakes within the terms of an economy of sacrifice, but this is by sacrificing sacrifice understood as commerce occurring within finite bounds. There is *merces*, wages, merchandizing if not mercantilism; there is payment, but not commerce if commerce presupposes the *finite* and reciprocal exchange of wages, merchandise, or reward. The dissymmetry signifies that different economy of sacrifice in terms of which Christ, still talking about the eye, about the right and the left, about breaking up a pair or pairing up, will say a little later:

> Ye have heard that it hath been said, An eye for an eye (*oculum pro oculo / ophthalmon anti ophthalmou*), and a tooth for a tooth:
> But I say unto you, That ye resist not evil (*non resistere malo / mē antistēnai tō ponerō*): but whosoever shall smite thee on thy right cheek, turn to him the other also. (5: 38-39)

Does this commandment reconstitute the parity of the pair rather than breaking it up, as we just suggested? No it doesn't, it interrupts the parity and symmetry, for instead of *paying back* the slap on the cheek (right cheek for left cheek, eye for eye), one is to *offer* the other cheek. It is a matter of suspending the strict economy of exchange, of payback, of giving and giving back, of the "one lent for every one borrowed," of that hateful form of circulation that involves reprisal, vengeance, returning blow for blow, settling scores. So what are we to make of this economical symmetry of exchange, of give and take and of paying back that is implied when it is said, a little further on, that God who sees in secret, will reward you or pay you back for it (*reddet tibi*)? The logic that requires a suspension of the reciprocity of vengeance and that commands us not to resist evil is naturally the logic, the *logos* itself, which is life and truth, namely, Christ who, as goodness that forgets itself as Patočka says, teaches love for one's enemies. For it is precisely in this passage that he says: "Love your enemies . . . pray for them which . . . persecute you," etc. (*Diligite inimicos vestros / agapate tous ekhthrous humōn*) (5: 44). It is more than ever necessary to quote the Latin or Greek, if only to remind us of the remark made by Carl Schmitt when, in Chapter 3 of *The Concept of the Political*, he emphasizes the fact that *inimicus* is not *hostis* in Latin and *ekhthros* is not *polemios* in Greek. This allows him to conclude that Christ's teaching concerns the love that we must show to our private enemies, to those we would be tempted to hate through personal or subjective passion, and not to public enemies. (Schmitt recognizes in passing that the distinctions between *inimicus* and *hostis* and between *ekhthros* and *polemios* have no strict equivalent in other languages, at least not in German.) Christ's teaching would thus be moral or psychological, even metaphysical, but not political. This is important for Schmitt, for whom war waged against a determinate enemy (*hostis*), a war or hostility that doesn't presuppose any hate, would be the condition of possibility of politics. As he reminds us, no Christian politics ever advised the West to love the Muslims who invaded Christian Europe.

Among other things this raises again the question of a Christian politics, one that conforms to the Gospels. For Schmitt, but in a very different sense from Patočka, a Christian or European-Christian politics seems to be possible. The modern sense of the political itself would be tied to such a possibility inasmuch as political concepts are secularized theologico-political concepts. But for that to make sense one must presuppose that Schmitt's reading of "love your enemies" preempts all discussion or, as we might say, all ethno-philological debate, since the war waged against the Muslims, to cite but a single case, was a political fact, in Schmitt's sense, and it confirmed the existence of a Christian politics, of a

coherent intention that was in genuine agreement with the Gospel
of Matthew, capable of bringing all Christians and the whole
Church together in a spirit of consensus. But that can be called into
question, just as we can find ourselves perplexed by the reading of
"love your enemies and pray for those who persecute you." For
the text says:

> Ye have heard that it hath been said, Thou shalt love
> thy neighbor, and hate thine enemy.
> But I say unto you, Love your enemies, bless them
> that curse you, do good to them that hate you, and pray
> for them which despitefully use you, and persecute you.
> (5: 43-44)

When Jesus says "Ye have heard that it hath been said, Thou
shalt love thy neighbor, and hate thine enemy," he refers in particular to Leviticus 19: 15-18, at least in the first part of the sentence
("Thou shalt love thy neighbor") if not the second ("hate thine
enemy"). There it is said, in fact, "Thou shalt love thy neighbor
as thyself." But in the first place vengeance is already condemned
in Leviticus and the text doesn't say "hate thine enemy." In the
second place, since it defines the neighbor in the sense of fellow
creature [*congénère*], as a member of the same ethnic group (*'amith*),
the sphere of the political in Schmitt's sense is already in play. It
would seem difficult to keep the potential opposition between one's
neighbor and one's enemy within the sphere of the private. The
passage from Leviticus sets forth a certain concept of justice. God
is speaking to Moses, to whom he has just given a series of prescrip-
tions concerning sacrifice and payment, and, it needs to be emphasized, he forbids revenge:

> I am the Lord.
> Ye shall do no unrighteousness in judgment: thou shalt
> not respect the person of the poor, nor honor the person
> of the mighty: but in righteousness shalt thou judge thy
> neighbor. Thou shalt not go up and down as a talebearer
> among the people: neither shalt thou stand against the
> blood of thy neighbor: I am the Lord.

> Thou shalt not hate thy brother in thine heart: thou
> shalt in any wise rebuke thy neighbor, and not suffer sin
> upon him.
> *Thou shalt not avenge*, nor bear any grudge against the
> children of thy people, but thou shalt love thy neighbor
> as thyself: I am the Lord. (Leviticus 19: 15-18)

If one's neighbor is here one's *congener*, someone from *my* community, from the same people or nation (*'amith*), then the person
who can be opposed to him or her (not in Leviticus but indeed in
the Gospel) is the non-neighbor not as private enemy but as for-
eigner, as member of another nation, community, or people. That
runs counter to Schmitt's interpretation: the frontier between *inimicus* and *hostis* would be more permeable than he wants to believe.
This involves the conceptual and practical possibility of founding
politics or of forming a rigorous concept of political specificity by
means of a type of dissociation: not only that between the public
and private but also between public existence and the passion or
shared community affect that links each of its members to the
others, as with members of the same family, the same ethnic,
national, or linguistic community, etc. Is national or nationalist
affect, or community affect, political in itself, or not? Is it public
or private, according to Schmitt? It would be difficult to answer
the question, and to do so would require a new elaboration of the
problematic.

What follows immediately the "Love your enemies" in the Gospel of Matthew refers once again to wages or salary (*mercedem/
misthon*). Once again, and once already, for the question of remuneration will permeate the discourse on God the Father who sees
in secret and who will reward you (by implication with a salary).
We need to distinguish between two types of salary: one of retribution, equal exchange, within a circular economy; the other of absolute surplus value, heterogeneous to outlay or investment. Two
seemingly heterogeneous economies therefore, but in any case two
types of wages, two types of *merces* or *misthos*. And the opposition
between the mediocre wages of retribution or exchange and the
noble salary that is obtained through disinterested sacrifice or

through the gift also points to an opposition between two peoples,
ours, to whom Christ is speaking, and the others, who are referred
to as *ethnici* or *ethnikoi*, the races, therefore, in short the peoples,
those who are only peoples, collectivities (*goyim* in Chouraqui's
French translation, *pagans* in Grosjean's and Léturmy's Bibliothèque de la Pléiade version). Let us not forget the use of the word
"pagan," for it will shortly further advance our reading. Here is
the end of Chapter 5 of the Gospel according to Matthew:

> But I say unto you, Love your enemies, bless them
> that curse you, do good to them that hate you, and pray
> for them which despitefully use you, and persecute you;
> That ye may be the children of your Father which is in
> heaven: for he maketh his sun to rise on the evil and on
> the good, and sendeth rain on the just and on the unjust.
> For if ye love them which love you, what reward have ye
> (*Si enim diligitis eos qui vos diligunt, quam mercedem habe-
> bitis? / ean gar agapēsete tous agapōntas humas, tina misthon
> ekhete*)? do not even the publicans the same? (44-46)

Something passes from one father to another but authentic filia-
tion is reinstated ("that ye may be children of your Father"); it
occurs on condition that there is a gift, a love *without reserve*. If
you love only those who love you and to the extent that they
love you, if you hold so strictly to this symmetry, mutuality, and
reciprocity, then you give nothing, no love, and the reserve of
your wages will be like a tax that is imposed or a debt that is
repaid, like the acquittal of a debt. In order to deserve or expect
an infinitely higher salary, one that goes beyond the perception of
what is due, you have to give without taking account and love
those who don't love you. It is here that reference is made to
"ethnic groups" or "pagans":

> And if you salute your brethren only, what do ye more
> than others? Do not even the Gentiles (*ethnici/ethnikoi*) so?[6]

6. In French, *les païens*, "pagans," "heathens." "Gentiles" is from the Revised
Standard Version; King James repeats "publicans" (*telōnai*) as in verse 46. Both
exist in different versions of the Greek.—Trans. note.

This infinite and dissymmetrical economy of sacrifice is opposed to that of the scribes and pharisees, to the old law in general, and to that of heathen ethnic groups or gentiles (*goyim*); it refers on the one hand to the Christian as against the Judaic, on the other hand to the Judeo-Christian as against the rest. It always presupposes a calculation that claims to go beyond calculation, beyond the totality of the calculable as a finite totality of the same. There is an economy, but it is an economy that integrates the renunciation of a calculable remuneration, renunciation of merchandise or bargaining [*marchandage*], of economy in the sense of a retribution that can be measured or made symmetrical. In the space opened by this economy of what is without measure there emerges a new teaching concerning giving or alms that relates the latter to *giving back* or *paying back*, a yield [*rendement*] if you wish, a profitability [*rentabilité*] also, of course, but one that creatures cannot calculate and must leave to the appreciation of *the father as he who sees in secret*. Starting from Chapter 6 of the same Gospel, the theme of justice is remarked upon if not marked out explicitly, or it is at least appealed to and named as that which must be practiced without being marked or remarked upon. One must be just without being noticed for it. To want to be noticed means wanting recognition and payment in terms of a calculable salary, in terms of thanks [*remerciement*] or recompense. On the contrary one must give, alms for example, without knowing, or at least by giving with one hand without the other hand knowing, that is, without having it known, without having it known by other men, in secret, without counting on recognition, reward, or remuneration. Without even having it known to oneself. The dissociation between right and left again breaks up the pair, the parity or pairing, the symmetry between, or homogeneity of, two economies. In fact it inaugurates sacrifice. But an infinite calculation supersedes the finite calculating that has been renounced. God the Father, who sees in secret, will pay back your salary, and on an infinitely greater scale.

Have things become clearer? Perhaps, except for the divine light, upon whose secret light should not be shed:

> Take heed that ye do not your alms before men, to be seen of them: otherwise ye have no reward of your Father which is in heaven.
>
> Therefore when thou doest thine alms, do not sound a trumpet before thee, as the hypocrites do in the synagogues and in the streets, that they may have glory of men. Verily I say unto you, They have their reward.
>
> But when thou doest alms, let not thy left hand know what thy right hand doeth:
>
> That thine alms may be in secret; and thy Father which seeth in secret himself shall reward thee openly. (Matthew 6: 1-4)

This promise is repeated several times in a similar form, whether it concerns alms, prayer, or fasting (6: 6, 17-18). The clarity of divine lucidity penetrates everything yet keeps within itself the most secret of secrets. In order to eschew idolatrous or iconistic simplicisms, that is, visible images and ready-made representations, it might be necessary to understand this sentence ("and thy Father which seeth in secret . . . shall reward thee") as something other than a proposition concerning God, this subject, entity, or X who on the one hand would already exist, and who, on the other hand, what is more, would be endowed with attributes such as paternity and the power to penetrate secrets, to see the invisible, to see in me better than I, to be more powerful and more intimate with me than myself. We should stop thinking about God as someone, over there, way up there, transcendent, and, what is more—into the bargain, precisely—capable, more than any satellite orbiting in space, of seeing into the most secret of the most interior places. It is perhaps necessary, if we are to follow the traditional Judeo-Christiano-Islamic injunction, but also at the risk of turning it against that tradition, to think of God and of the name of God without such idolatrous stereotyping or representation. Then we might say: God is the name of the possibility I have of keeping a secret that is visible from the interior but not from the exterior. Once such a structure of conscience exists, of being-with-oneself, of speaking, that is, of producing invisible sense, once I have within me, *thanks to the invisible word as such,* a witness that others cannot see, and who is therefore *at the same time other than me and more intimate with me than myself,* once I can have a secret relationship with myself and not tell everything, once there is secrecy and secret witnessing within me, then what I call God exists, (there is) what I call God in me, (it happens that) I call myself God—a phrase that is difficult to distinguish from "God calls me," for it is on that condition that I can call myself or that I am called in secret. God is in me, he is the absolute "me" or "self," he is that structure of invisible interiority that is called, in Kierkegaard's sense, subjectivity. And he is made manifest, he manifests his nonmanifestation when, in the structures of the living or the entity, there appears in the course of phylo- and ontogenetic history, the possibility of secrecy, however differentiated, complex, plural, and overdetermined it be; that is, when there appears the desire and power to render absolutely invisible and to constitute within oneself a witness of that invisibility. That is the history of God and of the name of God as the history of secrecy, a history that is at the same time secret and without any secrets. Such a history is also an economy.

Another economy? Perhaps the same one in simulacrum, an economy that is ambiguous enough to seem to integrate noneconomy. In its essential instability the same economy seems sometimes faithful to and sometimes accusing or ironic with respect to the role of Christian sacrifice. It begins by denouncing an offering that appears too calculating still; one that would renounce earthly, finite, accountable, exterior, visible wages (*merces*), one that would exceed an economy of retribution and exchange (the *re-merciement*) only to capitalize on it by gaining a profit or surplus value that was infinite, heavenly, incalculable, interior, and secret. This would be a sort of secret calculation that would continue to wager on the gaze of God who sees the invisible and sees in my heart what I decline to have seen by my fellow humans.

The hyperbolic form of this internal critique of Christianity, that is at same time evangelical and heretical, is illustrated in

a short pamphlet by Baudelaire, "The Pagan School" (1852).[7] In
a few intemperate pages, his verve and anger project a poetics, a
morality, a religion, and a philosophy. First among the accused
are some unnamed writers (probably Banville and others like Le-
conte de Lisle and Gautier, who celebrated models of Greek culture). Declaring himself against the cult of form and plasticity of
those he calls the neo-pagans, who are at the same time idolatrous,
materialist, and formalist, Baudelaire warns against the prostitu-
tion of those who kneel before the aestheticism of representation,
against the materialism of the image, of appearances and of idola-
try, against the literal exteriority of appearing (elsewhere he
doesn't fail to do the contrary, according to a controlled paradoxol-
ogy whose "logical" program cannot be elaborated here). Speaking
of alms a little in the manner of Matthew's Gospel, he ends up
by recounting a story of counterfeit money that is simpler, more
impoverished, and less perverse than "Counterfeit Money,"[8] but
still close enough to call for an analysis that would link the two
texts in a series. And he "excuses the suppression of the object":

> Impossible to take a step, to speak a word without stum-
> bling into something pagan. . . . And you, miserable neo-
> pagans, what are you doing if not the same thing? . . .
> Apparently you have lost your soul somewhere. . . . To
> dismiss passion and reason is to kill literature. To repudi-
> ate the efforts of a preceding society, Christian and philo-
> sophic, is to commit suicide. . . . To surround oneself
> exclusively with the charms of material art is to run the
> risk of damnation. For a long time, a very long time, you
> will be able to see, love and feel only the beautiful, and
> nothing but the beautiful. I am using the word in a re-
> stricted sense. The world will appear to you only in its

7. Charles Baudelaire, "The Pagan School," in Lois Boe Hyslop and Francis
E. Hyslop, Jr., eds. and trans., *Baudelaire as Literary Critic*. University Park: Penn-
sylvania State University Press, 1964.
8. The allusion to the counterfeiter in "The Pagan School" was not taken into
account in my reading of "Counterfeit Money" (cf. *Given Time. 1. Counterfeit
Money*, trans. Peggy Kamuf (Chicago: University of Chicago Press, 1992).

material form. . . . May religion and philosophy come one day as if compelled by the cry of a despairing soul. Such will always be the fate of madmen who see in nature only forms and rhythms. Even philosophy will at first appear to them as only an interesting game. . . . His soul [that of the child so corrupted], constantly excited and unappeased, goes about the world, the busy, toiling world . . . like a prostitute crying: Plastic! Plastic! The plastic—that frightful word gives me goose flesh—the plastic has poisoned him, and yet he can live only by this poison. . . . I understand the rage of iconoclasts and Moslems against images. I admit all the remorse of Saint Augustine for the too great pleasure of the eyes. The danger is so great that I excuse the suppression of the object. The folly of art is equal to the abuse of the mind. The creation of one of these two supremacies results in foolishness, hardness of heart and in enormous pride and egoism. I recall having heard an artist, who was a practical joker and who had received a false coin, say on one occasion: I shall keep it for some poor person. The wretch took an infernal pleasure in robbing the poor and in enjoying at the same time the benefit of a reputation for charity. I heard someone else say: Why don't the poor wear gloves to beg? They would make a fortune. And another: Don't give anything to that one; his rags don't fit well; they aren't very becoming to him. . . . The time is not distant when it will be understood that every literature that refuses to walk hand in hand with science and philosophy is a homicidal and suicidal literature. ("The Pagan School," 74-77)

This discourse seems to be of a piece and it is certainly less intricate than "Counterfeit Money." But it still lends itself to two readings. The stakes of evangelical spiritualism that continue to be raised are at constant risk of having their bluff called. In the salary promised in heaven by the Father who sees in secret and will pay it back, "The Pagan School" can always unmask a sort of sublime and secret calculation, that of him who seeks to "win paradise economically" as the narrator of "Counterfeit Money" puts it. The moment the gift, however generous it be, is infected with the slightest hint of calculation, the moment it takes account of knowledge [*connaissance*] or recognition [*reconnaissance*], it falls within the ambit of an economy: it exchanges, in short it gives counterfeit money, since it gives in exchange for payment. Even if it gives "true" money, the alteration of the gift into a form of calculation immediately destroys the value of the very thing that is given; it destroys it as if from the inside. The money may keep its value but it is no longer given as such. Once it is tied to remuneration (*merces*), it is counterfeit because it is mercenary and mercantile; even if it is real. Whence the double "suppression of the object" that can be inferred by slightly displacing Baudelaire's formulation: as soon as it is calculated (starting from the simple intention of giving *as such*, starting from sense, knowledge, and whatever takes recognition into account), the gift suppresses the object (of the gift). It denies it as such. In order to avoid this negation or destruction at all costs, one must proceed to *another* suppression of the object: that of keeping in the gift only the giving, the act of giving and intention to give, not the given which in the end doesn't count. One must give without knowing, without knowledge or recognition, without *thanks* [*remerciement*]: without anything, or at least without any object.

The critique or polemic of "The Pagan School" would have the virtue of *demystification*. The word is no longer fashionable but it does seem to impose itself in this case, does it not? It is a matter of unfolding the mystagogical hypocrisy of a secret, putting on trial a fabricated mystery, a contract that has a secret clause, namely, that, seeing in secret, God will pay back infinitely more; a secret that we accept all the more easily since God remains the witness of every secret. He shares and *he knows*. We have to *believe* that he knows. This knowledge at the same time founds and destroys the Christian concepts of responsibility and justice and their "object." The genealogy of responsibility that Nietzsche refers to in *The Genealogy of Morals* as "the long history of the origin of responsibility (*Verantwortlichkeit*)" also describes the history of moral and religious conscience—a history of cruelty and sacrifice, of the holocaust even (these are Nietzsche's words), of fault as debt or obligation (*Schuld*, that "cardinal idea," that *Hauptbegriff* of morality), a history of the economy of "the contractual relationship" between creditors (*Gläubiger*) and debtors (*Schuldner*). These relations appear as soon as there exist subjects under law in general (*Rechtssubjekte*), and they point back in turn "to the primary forms of purchase, sale, barter, and trade."[9]

Sacrifice, vengeance, cruelty—all that is inscribed through the genesis of responsibility and moral conscience. "The categorical imperative" of "old Kant" reeks of cruelty (72-73). But Nietzsche's diagnosis of cruelty is at the same time aimed at economy, speculation, and commercial trafficking (buying and selling) in the institution of morality and justice. It is also aimed at the "objectivity" of the object: " 'everything has its price, *all* can be paid for'." This was "the oldest and most naive moral canon of *justice*, the beginning of all 'kindness,' of all 'equity,' of all 'goodwill,' of all 'objectivity' in the world" (80).

For Nietzsche goes so far as to take into account, as it were, the moment when this justice integrates what cannot be rendered solvent, the unacquittable, the absolute. He thus takes into account that which exceeds economy as exchange, and the commerce of *re-merciement*. But instead of crediting that to pure goodness, to faith, or the infinite gift, he reveals in it, at the same time as the suppression of the object, a self-destruction of justice by means of grace. That is the properly Christian moment as self-destruction of justice:

> The justice which began with the maxim, "Everything can be paid off, everything must be paid off," ends with connivance (*durch die Finger zu sehn*) at the escape of those who cannot pay to escape—it ends, like every good thing on earth, by *destroying itself* [what is translated as "destroying itself" is literally *sich selbst aufhebend*—and Nietzsche adds the emphasis: by "raising itself or by substituting for itself," Christian justice denies itself and so

9. Friedrich Nietzsche, *The Genealogy of Morals*, vol. 13 in *The Complete Works of Friedrich Nietzsche*, ed. Dr. Oscar Levy (New York: Gordon Press, 1974), 70.

conserves itself in what seems to exceed it; it remains what it ceases to be, a cruel economy, a commerce, a contract involving debt and credit, sacrifice and vengeance]. The self-destruction of Justice (*Diese Selbstaufhebung der Gerechtigkeit*)! we know the pretty name it calls itself—*Grace (Gnade)!* it remains, as is obvious, the privilege (*Vorrecht*) of the strongest, better still, their super-law (*sein Jenseits des Rechts*). (83-84)

In its *Selbstaufhebung* justice remains a privilege, *Gerechtigkeit* remains a *Vorrecht* as that which is *Jenseits des Rechts*. That obliges us to think about what the *Selbst* represents in this *Selbstaufhebung* in terms of the constitution of the self in general, through this secret nucleus of responsibility.

In questioning a certain concept of repression (*Zurückschiebung*, 110) that moralizes the mechanism of debt[10] in moral duty and in bad conscience, in conscience as guilt, one might develop further the hyperbolization of such a repression (by bringing it to bear upon what Patočka says about Christian repression). This sacrificial *hubris* is what Nietzsche calls the "stroke of genius called Christianity." It is what takes this economy to its excess in the sacrifice of Christ for love of the debtor; it involves the same economy of sacrifice, the same sacrifice of sacrifice:

> . . . that paradoxical and awful expedient, through which a tortured humanity has found a temporary alleviation, that stroke of genius called *Christianity* (*jenem Geniestreich des* Christentums):—God personally immolating himself for the debt of man, God paying himself personally out of a pound of his own flesh, God as the one being who can deliver man from what for man had become unacquittable (*unablösbar*)—the creditor (*der Gläubiger*) playing scapegoat for his debtor (*seinen Schuldner*), from *love* (can you believe it? [*sollte man's glauben?*]) from love of his debtor! . . . (111)

---

10. I have approached these passages from *The Genealogy of Morals* from a different perspective in *The Post Card: From Socrates to Freud and Beyond*, trans. Alan Bass (Chicago: University of Chicago Press, 1987) notably 263-65.

If there is such a thing as this "stroke of genius," it only comes about at the instant of the infinite sharing of the secret. If, on the basis of a thaumaturgical secret, like a technique derived from some capability, or a ruse that depends on a special knowhow, one were able to attribute it to someone or something called "Christianity," one would have to envelop another secret within it: the reversal and infinitization that confers on God, on the other or on the name of God, the responsibility for that which remains more secret than ever, the irreducible experience of belief, between credit and faith, the *believing* suspended between the credit [*créance*] of the creditor ([*créancier*] *Gläubiger*) and the credence ([*croyance*] *Glauben*) of the believer [*croyant*]. How can one *believe* this history of *credence* or *credit?* That is what Nietzsche asks, *in fine,* what he asks himself or has asked by another, by the specter of his discourse. Is this a false or counterfeit question, a rhetorical question as one says in English? For what makes a rhetorical question possible can sometimes disturb the structure of it.

As often happens, the call of or for the question, and the request that echoes through it, takes us further than the response. The question, the request, and the appeal *must* indeed have begun, since the eve of their awakening, by receiving accreditation from the other: by being believed. Nietzsche must indeed believe he knows what believing means, unless he means it is all make-believe [*à moins qu'il n'entende le faire accroire*].